W9-AEB-441

Eco-Business

Eco-Business

A Big-Brand Takeover of Sustainability

Peter Dauvergne and Jane Lister

The MIT Press
Cambridge, Massachusetts
London, England

MIT Press books may be purchased at special quantity discounts for business or sales promotional use. For information, please email special_sales@ mitpress.mit.edu or write to Special Sales Department, The MIT Press, 55 Hayward Street, Cambridge, MA 02142.

Set in Sabon by the MIT Press. Printed on recycled paper and bound in the United States of America.

Library of Congress Cataloging-in-Publication Data

Dauvergne, Peter.
Eco-business : a big-brand takeover of sustainability / Peter Dauvergne and Jane Lister.
    pages   cm
Includes bibliographical references and index.
ISBN 978-0-262-01876-0 (hardcover : alk paper)
1. Sustainable development—Environmental aspects. 2. Branding (Marketing) I. Lister, Jane. II. Title.
HC79.E5.D346   2013
658.4'083—dc23
2012026833

10   9   8   7   6   5   4   3   2   1

for our fathers

Contents

Acknowledgments   ix

1   **The Politics of "Big-Brand Sustainability"**   **1**
The Rise of Eco-Business   4
The Business of Eco-Business   10
The Governance Power of Eco-Business   16
Partnering with Power   19
The Limits of Eco-Business   22
A Branded World   26

2   **The Eco-Business Setting**   **29**
The Rise of Global Environmentalism   30
The Growth of Big Retail   33
Globalization of Production   42
Scarcity and Instability   46
The Emerging Middle Class   48
Competing for the World's Eco-Business   52

3   **The Eco-Business Market Advantage**   **55**
Bottom-Line Eco-Efficiency   56
Top-Line Growth   74
Choosing Environment *and* Profit?   80

4   **Eco-Business Tools of Supply-Chain Power**   **83**
Capturing Supply-Chain Value   84
Managing Supply-Chain Risks   87

Eco-Business Tools for Supply-Chain Control   93
The Rising Power of Eco-Business   110

5   **The Supply-Chain Eco-Business of Brand Growth**   **113**
Securing Resources   114
Coercing and Cooperating for Added Value   122
Rolling Back Prices   125
"Sustainable" Shipping   127
Connecting with Consumers   129
Scaling Up Eco-Business   132

6   **Eco-Business Governance**   **135**
Big Brands' Governing Authority   137
Leading and Guiding Business   145
Keeping Pace with the Global Economy   154
Ecological Sustainability   158
Engaging with Eco-Business   160

Notes   163
Further Readings   183
Index   191

Acknowledgments

Any book about "brands" and "sustainability" is going to be contentious. Opinions on the value of corporate sustainability are sharp and varied, and for many the topic quickly feels personal—and rightly so. Few will escape feeling part of what we discuss in this book—certainly not anyone who has ever shopped at Costco, or drunk Starbucks coffee, or used an iPod, an iPad, or an iPhone. The support of family, friends, and colleagues allowed us to navigate through a storm of arguments and counterarguments as we wrote and rewrote the book. For some, the world's biggest companies are mainstreaming and scaling up sustainability. For others, expecting companies such as Walmart and McDonald's to "save the world" is like expecting the Mafia to bring law and order.

Many people gave feedback on various drafts. A special thank you to our academic team at the Liu Institute for Global Issues, including doctoral students Kate Neville, Sara Elder, and Jennifer Allan, postdoctoral fellow Genevieve LeBaron, and research assistant Hannah Griffiths. The stellar staff at the Liu Institute deserve our gratitude, too: Patty Gallivan, Sally Reay, Timothy Shew, and Julie Wagemakers. We are also appreciative of the time and advice from several expert practitioners, including Coro Strandberg, and especially Liu Institute Distinguished Fellow Linda Coady.

We also want to acknowledge the scores of astute questions and comments when presenting our research to diverse audiences, including those at the Nicholas School of the Environment at Duke University, the Carleton School of Public Policy and Administration, the Institute for Resources, Environment and Sustainability at the University of British Columbia, the Schatz Energy Research Center and Environment and Community Program at Humboldt State University, the National Autonomous University of Mexico, and the Vancouver Institute.

The book would not have been possible without the vision and support of Clay Morgan at the MIT Press. We are also thankful to the anonymous peer reviewers for the press who took the time to offer many useful suggestions.

Finally, we extend deep gratitude to our families, in particular to Jane's father, Bruce Lister, for his unfailing eagerness to read, edit, and praise each evolving draft; to Peter's wife, Catherine, for her insight and good humor; and to Peter's daughter Nina for asking the right questions (What is sustainability? Should I shop at Walmart?) at just the right time.

1

The Politics of "Big-Brand Sustainability"

Zero waste. 100 percent renewable energy. Zero toxics. 100 percent sustainable sourcing. Zero deforestation. These are just some of the grand promises that multinational companies such as Walmart, Nestlé, Nike, McDonald's, and Coca-Cola are now making as they claim to lead a corporate charge toward "sustainability." "We're integrating sustainability principles and practices into everything we do," Nike tells us boldly.[1]

What is going on? Why are these companies making such promises? Why do they seem to be accelerating their efforts? Is this merely crafty marketing? Are they using feel-good rhetoric to placate governments, activists, and consumers? Some of what we are seeing is definitely "greenwash" and business as usual. But, as this book will reveal, these iterations of "corporate sustainability" have more powerful drivers and motives, and more varied consequences, than previous iterations, which tended toward peripheral, one-off, reputation-saving responses. Now, leading-brand companies are racing to adopt sustainability in order to enhance their growth and control within the global economy. These "big brands" are defining sustainability and implementing it through their operations and supply chains to gain competitive advantages and increase sales and profits.

What we call "eco-business"—taking over the idea of sustainability and turning it into a tool of business control and growth that projects an image of corporate social responsibility—is proving to be a powerful strategy for corporations in a rapidly globalizing economy marked by financial turmoil and a need for continual strategic repositioning. It is also enhancing the credibility and influence of these companies in states, in civil society, in supply chains, and in retail markets. And it is shifting the power balance within the global political arena from states as the central rule makers and enforcers of environmental goals toward big-brand retailers and manufacturers acting to use "sustainability" to protect their private interests.[2]

Eco-business is likely to keep rising in importance as a global force of change—a trend that global governance analysts and practitioners will have to watch closely. Some are applauding this trend, seeing it as valuable for the mainstreaming and scaling up of sustainability that global solutions will require. Executives of big-brand companies also are making this case, arguing they are "sustainability leaders" and that states now are the "laggards." They are quick to provide example after example of savings, efficiencies, social responsibility, and more transparency and accountability within supply chains. On the surface, the benefits of eco-business do seem to be advancing environmental improvements—and, as we will see later, many governments and environmental groups are now rushing to partner with big brands. For those wanting to hear some good news for a change, it is easy to find the apparent gains reassuring.

Can eco-business halt the rise and the harmful social consequences of global ecological loss? The answer in this book is a forceful "no." Eco-business is fundamentally aiming for sustainability of big business, not sustainability of people and the planet. It is not about absolute limits to natural resources or waste sinks; nor is it about the security of communities or family businesses. As will be introduced in chapter 2 and illustrated in the rest of the book, it is largely about more efficiently controlling supply chains and effectively navigating a globalizing world economy to increase brand consumption. Some good can come out of eco-business. Indeed, one source of its power as a marketing and management tool, and one reason why it is a force that will keep growing in importance within global governance, is that it has the capacity to achieve clear and measurable economic gains. Chapter 3 (the topic of which is the value of eco-business for achieving efficiencies and scaling up eco-markets) confirms this. So does chapter 4, the subject of which is the use of eco-business tools—such as supply-chain tracing, supplier auditing, and eco-labeling—to enhance supply-chain transparency, control, and risk management. Even chapter 5, on eco-business' use in supply chains to promote brand growth, shows its utility for resource security, quality and productivity gains, and price management.

Though eco-business is good for business and for the economy, it has limits as a force of environmental protection and social justice—limits that are hidden behind corporate sustainability claims and promises, and that arise directly from the explanation of why and how big brands are adopting it. As this book will reveal, much of what big brands are doing involves defining and using sustainability as a business tool in ways that are actually increasing risks and adding to an ever-mounting global crisis. Part of the growing value of eco-business, moreover, is its capacity to help "roll back" consumer prices by shifting costs upstream onto those least likely to be able to afford them: small suppliers and low-paid labor. This is helping to stimulate consumption of retail goods even during economic downturns. Equally disquieting, eco-business is increasing the power of big-brand companies to sway nonprofit organizations, shape international codes and standards, and influence state regulations and institutions toward market interests. In view of all this, as chapter 6 will conclude, governments, environmental groups, and consumers have no choice but to engage with big-brand eco-business—something that will have to be done with eyes wide open about its limits and its overall consequences. True or "deep" sustainability requires restoring and protecting ecosystems and communities, and not, as every big brand is doing, first and foremost trying to use sustainability to enhance the efficiency of production and the quality of products to speed along growth.

The Rise of Eco-Business

Big brands *do not* call their efforts "eco-business," nor would one expect them to do so. Calling their efforts "sustainability" is helping them to control the global sustainability agenda. Putting this under the rubric of corporate social responsibility (CSR), or a triple bottom-line balance of environmental, social, and economic factors, casts their efforts in a win-win light: big corporations can be socially responsible *and* profit maximizing through what Michael Porter and Mark Kramer call "strategic CSR."[3] This book develops the concept of eco-business to help avoid some of the confusion that can arise from the many meanings of sustainability that range from small adjustments to transformative change—a confusion that corporations sometimes knowingly exploit to reassure governments and customers. The concept of eco-business also helps to emphasize that the principal motive behind the sustainability programs and policies of big brands is sustaining corporate growth. It also serves as a reminder that the focus of big brands is on gaining business advantages through primarily *environmental* efforts—and that these efforts may in some instances even harm workers and societies. Such a critical eye is essential to evaluate the many claims and promises that big-brand companies are now making under the banner of sustainability—and helps reveal why the business case for environmental programs is stronger than the business case for social ones.

Corporate efforts to find and gain environmental efficiencies date back decades.[4] The year 2005, however, saw a shift in the strategies of multinational retailers and manufacturers. General Electric launched its Ecomagination program, linking its growth strategy to clean water, energy, and technology, doubling its research-and-development budget to $1.5 billion, and setting a revenue target of $25 billion over the next five years from growing its green-design products—twice the rate of growth of total company revenue. Later that year, Walmart set aspirational goals of zero waste, carbon neutrality, and 100 percent sourcing of more responsibly produced products.

Big companies had made big sustainability promises before. Back in 2001, British Petroleum announced a "beyond petroleum" campaign. Ford had proclaimed in 1999 that it would "bring about the demise of the internal combustion engine," and had pledged in 2004 to spend half of its R&D budget on making its vehicles and its factories run cleaner. But these announcements were more about public relations than about the pursuit of business earnings and power. British Petroleum continued to rely on fossil fuels. And Ford stayed at the bottom of fuel-efficiency rankings for automakers.

The approach of General Electric and Walmart in 2005 was different. They were aiming to use corporate sustainability as a strategic tool to change practices to enhance financial strength and earnings potential—and thus to generate business value. This was more than just public relations or marketing. And it went beyond a risk-management program to protect a brand's reputation. Even more significant, this approach was not just looking to advance the bottom-line earnings through "eco-efficiency"[5]—an idea that was increasingly popular among companies after the 1992 Earth Summit in Rio de Janeiro—but was also striving to achieve top-line "green growth" by producing more goods from less resources and with less waste.

General Electric and Walmart were aiming to pursue environmental objectives through the entire corporate structure to gain competitive advantages and increase sales and profits. "Green is green," General Electric's chief executive officer, Jeffrey Immelt, explained when announcing Ecomagination. "We are launching Ecomagination not because it's trendy or moral but because it will accelerate our growth."[6] Before long, it wasn't just niche green brand leaders such as Body Shop, Patagonia, Ben & Jerry's, Whole Foods, and Interface Carpets that were embracing corporate sustainability. Big-box retailers and brand manufacturers in all consumer-goods sectors—from apparel and electronics to food and beverage to household and personal care products—were aiming to integrate eco-business into their guiding strategy. Today just about every big brand has a sustainability program. (Table 1.1 provides a sample.) And corporate executives are jockeying to position themselves as "thought-and-action" sustainability leaders who are setting a "future-friendly" direction for producers and consumers.[7]

Claims and Commitments

Almost every day, it seems, a big brand makes another sustainability claim or "commitment." Coca-Cola is promising water neutrality. McDonald's is promising sustainable sourcing of beef, coffee, fish, chicken, and cooking oil. Unilever is promising 100 percent sustainable agricultural sourcing and has set a deadline of 2020. H&M is promising to eliminate all hazardous chemicals from its apparel manufacturing, and Nestlé is promising zero deforestation from its activities. Adidas, Puma, and Nike are promising to eliminate all toxic discharges from

Table 1.1
Growth of eco-business programs. Sources: company reports (with goals partly quoted or paraphrased).

Company	Sustainability program	Year launched	Promises or goals
Sainsbury	20 by 20 Sustainability Plan	2011	Reach 20 sustainability targets for products, communities, and employees by 2020.
McDonald's	Sustainable Land Management Commitment	2011	Ensure that food served in McDonald's restaurants is sourced from certified sustainable sources.
Best Buy	Greener Together	2010	Encourage consumers to reduce, reuse, and trade in "end of life" electronics.
Procter & Gamble	Sustainability Vision	2010	Design products that maximize the conservation of resources.
Unilever	Sustainable Living Plan	2010	Decouple business growth from environmental impact.
PepsiCo	Performance with Purpose	2009	Deliver sustainable growth.
FedEx	Earth Smart	2009	Extend the depth and breadth of how sustainability is integrated into the company.
Nike	Considered Design	2008	Performance without compromising sustainability.
IBM	Smarter Planet	2008	Apply smart technology systems to sustainability solutions.

Table 1.1 (continued)

Company	Sustainability program	Year launched	Promises or goals
Starbucks	Shared Planet	2008	Aspire to environmental stewardship, ethical sourcing, and community involvement.
Marks & Spencer	Plan A	2007	Become the world's most sustainable retailer by 2015.
Coca-Cola	Live Positively	2007	Make a positive difference in the world.
Johnson & Johnson	Healthy Planet	2006	Safeguard the health of people and the planet.
Walmart	Sustainability Commitment	2005	Commit to zero waste, 100% renewable energy, and sustainable sourcing.
General Electric	Ecomagination	2005	Grow through clean energy, clean water, and clean technologies.

their factories, and Walmart, Tesco, Disney, Google, and Carrefour are promising to become carbon neutral.

And this is just a few of the claims and commitments. Dell now advertises that it offers free recycling of its products, and claims that it no longer allows "e-waste" to be exported to developing countries. IBM is claiming that it will reduce energy use worldwide through its "smart-grid" programs. And Procter & Gamble is setting—and claiming to meet—targets so that one day it will power all of its operations with 100 percent renewable energy, make all of its products with recyclable materials, and avoid sending any manufacturing and product waste to landfills.

Why Now?

What explains this recent rise of eco-business programs and promises? Companies are responding in part to state regulations and international laws. Some are also using sustainability language and programming to respond to environmental advocacy groups, consumers, investors, and employees as environmentalism broadens in diverse forms across diverse groups. But, as the next chapter will document in detail, the full explanation for the accelerating turn to eco-business must look at how the above factors are converging with changes in the world economy. These changes include the rise of global retailing, as well as growing populations and resource scarcities, high and volatile commodity prices, the 2007–2009 global economic downturn, and escalating ecological stressors such as climate change. Especially important for encouraging and enabling the increasing use of eco-business as a tool of corporate growth has been the well-documented globalization of production and the shift toward consumer goods moving along lengthening, dynamic supply chains through the surging economies of China, Brazil, and India.

The shift toward manufacturing and purchasing in China is particularly notable. To remain competitive all multinational corporations have been moving away from using home suppliers and owning foreign factories and toward working with thousands of small and medium-size suppliers worldwide. Walmart reports that it has about 20,000 suppliers in China alone. China is now central to the world retail economy, with Chinese manufacturers still expanding at home as well as outsourcing more and more to developing countries in search of cheaper labor, natural resources, and infrastructure. Moving into China is also part of an effort by big brands to reach the country's rapidly growing middle class. By mid 2010, Walmart had 189 stores in 101 cities across China: a steady increase after opening its first Supercenter and Sam's Club in Shenzhen in 1996. Carrefour has announced that it will add 20–25 stores a year indefinitely. H&M is opening new outlets every week. IKEA is working to more than double its number of stores to 17. Starbucks is planning to expand from 459 stores (in 2010) to 1,500 stores by 2015. And this is just a sampling of big brands' expansion plans.

China's rise is creating some new dependencies and vulnerabilities for big brands. For example, by 2011, although having only 30 percent of global reserves, China was mining and refining at least 95 percent of the world's rare earth metals (seventeen elements that are needed to make a wide variety of products, ranging from Apple's iPhone to Toyota's Prius). The Chinese government has not been afraid to exercise this power—in 2010 it enforced a two-month ban on rare earth shipments to Japan during a territorial dispute.

These changes in the world economy are pushing big brands to search for greater efficiencies and resource security. They are looking to find better ways to maintain quality and reliable supplies within lower-cost but higher-risk global supply chains. And they are launching new growth strategies to capture markets in high-growth emerging economies. Eco-business, more and more big brands are finding, is an effective way to control supply chains, pursue efficiencies and competitive advantages, and generate business value (e.g., reputation, sales, profits, and growth).

The Business of Eco-Business

Eco-business efforts do vary across product segments, sectors, countries, and companies, from determined and sustained to weak and ad hoc. Many factors contribute to differences across and between manufacturers and retailers. These include the

origins and size of firms, the legal context of the primary operations, the technological complexity of the main products, and
the intricacy of supply chains. Inconsistencies of commitments
and actions continue within big-brand companies, too, leading to confusing proclamations that certain companies (e.g.,
Walmart and Coca-Cola) represent the best and the worst in
the world.

However, what is consistent across all the big brands is how
eco-business is helping to improve product-design and production processes and to turn waste streams into profit streams.
Measured on the basis of per unit of output, energy, water,
material use, and waste output intensity do seem to be lessening, if sometimes only fractionally. Big brands are winning
awards (with valuable reputational spinoffs) for these efforts.
In 2011, Unilever received the International Green Award for
"true innovation, thought leadership, and commitment to sustainable values that are integrated throughout the value chain."
The multi-stakeholder panel of judges praised the company for
being "an organization at the cutting edge of change and a
beacon that others aspire to follow."[8] *Newsweek* rated IBM
as America's greenest company in 2011. (Dell had ranked first
in 2010.) The magazine *Corporate Knights* ranked Johnson &
Johnson as the world's second "most sustainable company" in
2011—a position General Electric had held in 2010. Companies are also shining a spotlight on themselves with industry
awards. The business-led World Environment Center, for example, has awarded its International Corporate Achievement
in Sustainable Development prize to several of its member companies, including Marks & Spencer (2008), Coca-Cola (2009),
Walmart (2010), Nestlé (2011), and IBM (2012).

Much of what big brands are doing still involves enhancing the eco-efficiency of production to improve bottom-line
earnings. Hurdles such as managing up-front costs, payback

periods, access to capital, and uncertainty about how to measure the savings continue to challenge efficiency efforts. Yet finding ways to make a product with less resources, energy, and waste remains central to efforts to turn eco-business into savings and lower costs—and thus profit and competitive advantage. This became even more important during the global economic downturn of 2007–2009, and since then it has remained crucial for business success as brand companies look for efficiencies to help them ride out ongoing slowdowns in consumption. Striving for more eco-efficiency to improve the bottom line, however, is only part of what is encouraging eco-business. It is very much about enhancing the growth-oriented top line, too. (See chapter 3 on within-firm efforts and chapter 5 on external supply chains.) Nike, the world's largest apparel firm, sees great potential here: "[T]he opportunity is greater than ever for sustainability principles and practices to deliver business returns and become a driver of growth."[9]

The competition for revenues and markets is especially fierce in emerging economies, such as China and India, where companies are infusing traditional brands and products with "sustainability purpose" (e.g., hydration, mobility, connectivity, nourishment, and well-being) to capture new consumers. (See chapter 2 for details.) But eco-business is increasingly important in more mature markets, such as the United States, too. In 2008 alone, American consumers doubled their spending on "sustainable products and services" to about US$500 billion, according to the market-research firm Penn Schoen Berland. Big brands are extracting even greater bottom-line and top-line value, however, from the eco-business of supply chains.

Supply-Chain Management

Business analysts point to resilient and flexible supply chains as increasingly essential for the stability and profitability of multinational companies operating in a highly connected world economy prone to sudden shocks. An event such as the tsunami that struck Japan in 2011, for example, can reverberate quickly through supply systems, requiring big brands to find replacements quickly so as to keep stores stocked. Eco-business is helping retailers and brand manufacturers to enhance their resilience and their flexibility by better tracking the flow of inputs and products. Through eco-business, big brands are also enhancing their capacity to control and forecast future supply needs. This is especially valuable as retail manufacturing disperses to locations where costs are even lower, as resource scarcities intensify, and as commodity prices fluctuate sharply.

In addition, eco-business is helping big brands to work more directly with suppliers to improve the quality and security of supply. For example, multinational grocery firms and food manufacturers are providing advice, funding, and technical assistance to farmers all over the world in order to help them improve energy and water efficiency, reduce toxic chemicals, and cut down on waste. "Taking care of farmers' livelihoods," explains Steve Yucknut, Kraft's vice-president for sustainability, "ensures the stability of our supply chain and our long-term viability."[10]

Big-brand manufacturers are now competing hard to develop more efficient and durable supply structures. For those (e.g., Nokia and Microsoft) that require specialized components, the business gains of working more directly with suppliers can be immediate and significant if it lowers production costs. Multinational retailers, however, are working equally hard to achieve longer-term gains by implementing eco-business through their supply chains. A big-brand company can save millions, even billions, of dollars a year by reducing toxics, energy, materials, and packaging through its supply chains. "It is very good for business," a Walmart spokesman explains, "to drive waste out of our supply chain."[11] Walmart, as part of its agriculture strategy, is also working with local farmers in the developing world (e.g., their Direct Farm Program in China) to increase farm productivity and promote less wasteful practices to keep costs down.

Other mega-retailers, including Tesco, Safeway, Costco, and The Home Depot, are employing similar strategies. More and more, they are bypassing brokers and wholesalers to buy directly from suppliers. Some are going even further, requiring suppliers to deliver products to their stores—or, at least, to use the retailer's transportation system. This can enhance cost savings, inventory management, and distribution speed and, at the same time, enhance the power of buyers. Though most big-box retailers rely on partnerships with transport companies, many now also operate their own fleets of trucks. Walmart has more trucks on American roads than any other company.

Walmart and other companies portray such efforts as motivated by a "responsibility" to support small businesses and communities. Yet corporate financial interest is behind much of the advice, funding, and technical assistance within supply chains. Almost all of the big brands have treated their supply-chain operations as trade secrets in order to maintain competitive advantages and enhance control. Apple has not wanted Dell, Hewlett-Packard, and other competitors luring its suppliers away. Some firms swear suppliers to secrecy because they are sourcing products from the same factory as other companies, putting their private label on it, and then charging more than the other companies charge. Traditionally, keeping suppliers' names secret has left big-brand companies less exposed to poor supplier practices. And suppliers can't complain publicly if big brands squeeze them. Either they comply or they lose the contract. Still, in recent years some companies have been disclosing their supplier lists as part of risk management. In early

2012, for example, after suicides and employee protests at a supplier's plant in China, Apple announced that it would follow Dell and Hewlett-Packard and disclose 156 of its suppliers (representing 97 percent of its procurement expenditures).

At the same time, better Internet technologies, sensors, and software programs are making it easier and easier to track products through supply chains. Big brands are using this knowledge to report on environmental targets, to reassure customers, and to meet certification standards. Making their supply chains more accountable creates other business advantages, too. Gaining more control over suppliers can help them to improve their management of natural-resource inputs from regions experiencing political or economic instability, or when ecological problems (e.g., drought, infestation, over-harvesting, and natural disasters) put inputs at risk. Big-brand companies are also seeking to better document their supply-chain flows to avoid illegal inputs as well as put pressure on governments to shut down illegal competition. "Blood diamonds" and rainforest timber are pressing examples. Yet big-brand companies must also worry about the international trade of hundreds of thousands of seemingly minor commodities and product inputs. The illicit trade in honey, as we'll see in chapter 4, illustrates this well.

At least as important, big-brand companies are seeking greater control over suppliers in order to stabilize, and sometimes even lower, the costs—and thus the prices—of producing and transporting goods. One way big-brand companies exercise control is through sheer purchasing power. It is common for them to negotiate buying contracts that take up from 10 percent to 30 percent of a supplier's production capacity. To meet a large order, suppliers may even borrow funds to expand production or distribution capacity. For subsequent orders, if a big brand demands a discount, it can be hard, even impossible, for a small or medium-size supplier to refuse—at least without firing workers or going bankrupt. Instead, most suppliers look to cut costs. Sometimes this leads to innovation and to better environmental outcomes, such as less waste and more efficiency. Yet such pressure can also produce worse outcomes. Suppliers may cut corners, evade taxes, mistreat employees, and hide illegalities and poor practices by using subcontracted "shadow companies" and by falsifying audit reports.

The Governance Power of Eco-Business

The growing power of big brands within supply chains is not just about securing contracts to exchange goods and services for mutual profit. This type of market power is not new. Eco-business governance is equally about setting rules, establishing monitoring and reporting mechanisms, and punishing non-compliers. Some of this governance power is embedded in formal codes, policies, and legal contracts, but much of it is informal, sometimes maintained through coercive threats and sometimes through non-coercive financial opportunities.

The rising rule-making authority of big brands doesn't mean that suppliers have no power or autonomy. Many suppliers wield significant market control; others adopt dubious tactics to gain influence. The games these suppliers use to shave costs, disregard contracts, and conceal shady practices (e.g., double bookkeeping, switching ingredients, substituting lower-quality materials) could fill an entire book. Eco-business is giving big brands an edge, however, as they try to get suppliers to raise quality standards, implement just-in-time delivery, and reduce costs—all things that help discount retailers to roll back prices. Some of the influence big-brand companies have over suppliers comes from heavy-handed threats, such as to cancel or reduce purchase contracts or financing. But some of it comes from enticements, such as the prospect of a larger order.

Big-brand companies have long had noteworthy influence within supply chains. The "trend toward privatized global authority" started decades ago.[12] Many analysts since then have focused on understanding the rise and increasing acceptance of private eco-certification programs that mimic the regulatory role of public rule-making bodies. Although eco-certification systems offer supplemental governance capacity, such systems tend to be fractured, and implementation has been uneven and patchy at best. For example, although forest certification is one of the most well-developed international efforts to certify traded products, nearly 90 percent of certified forest is in the northern hemisphere; only 2 percent of under-regulated southern tropical forest is certified.[13]

The growth of eco-business is further concentrating the power and extending the governance scale and reach of private environmental authority. Transnational retail governance has the potential to produce global change faster than previous forms of environmental governance. Noting such capacity is not meant to suggest that this is good for societies or for ecosystems: without a doubt the politics of eco-business can harm local suppliers, developing economies, and the global environment. Identifying and better understanding this governing authority could, however, open up opportunities to channel it toward more social and ecological purposes.

The power of big brands across economies and cultures is unparalleled in history—and it is growing quickly. Procter & Gamble, PepsiCo, Nestlé, and other companies buy worldwide and sell into virtually every market. Nestlé sells about 10,000 different products, and in 2010 it netted $36 billion in profits on $115 billion in revenues. That works out to about a billion Nestlé products sold per day.[14] Big brands are striving in particular to reach consumers in developing economies where growth forecasts look highly promising. In India, Hindustan Unilever

(52 percent of which is owned by Unilever) already controls many of India's top consumer brands. In 2009, it added 500,000 new stores to the more than 6.1 million outlets it already had, achieving a growth in sales volume that year of 14 percent (a year in which retailers faced slower growth across most of the developed world).[15] In China, Procter & Gamble holds the top spot in every category of consumer products in which its brands compete. In 2010, P&G announced plans to invest an additional $1 billion or so in China over the next five years.

The reach and the influence of mass retailers such as Walmart, Tesco, and Best Buy are also increasing. Around 50 retailers are on the *Fortune* Global 500 list of the world's biggest companies by revenue turnover. Walmart is at the top. Walmart is now one of China's largest trading partners; only entire economies, including the United States, Japan, South Korea, Taiwan, and Germany, are ahead of it. And it is still growing quickly, with more than $440 billion in sales in fiscal year 2012 (ending January 31) across more than 10,000 outlets (under 69 different banners) in 27 countries. The fastest expansion is in the emerging economies. In the period 2005–2010, Walmart invested $3.8 billion in Brazil alone, and in 2011 it announced plans to add another 80 stores to the 450 it already had in Brazil. Carrefour (the world's second-biggest retailer, headquartered in France) has an even bigger presence in Brazil.

The governing reach of big brands is now deeply global. States can ignore, and often fall far short of meeting, international obligations. And companies everywhere tend to evade and soften government rules. Depending on the political context, they may use lawyers, bribes, or violence to do so. Yet a company that disobeys or ignores a big-brand chain leader runs the risk of being switched for a more compliant supplier.

The rising power and rule-making legitimacy of big brands within global supply chains is shifting power within sustainability governance toward the world's biggest retailers and brand manufacturers.[16] The rollout of eco-business, however, is ongoing and highly political: a negotiated and contested process involving multiple levels of shifting power relations and mechanisms of influence, from personal to structural. Through co-regulatory and co-participatory processes, as will be discussed in chapter 6, governments, activists, and consumers can engage eco-business to achieve particular goals. So can small businesses and suppliers. Some policy makers and activists think it may even be possible to leverage the eco-business of supply chains to increase the speed and the scale of environmental gains—and perhaps even keep pace with the rising stresses of the globalizing world economy. With this hope, a surprising number of nonprofit organizations and state agencies are now partnering with big-brand companies, despite knowing that this is legitimizing the influence and expansion of big brands and despite scores of risks and criticisms and compromises.

Partnering with Power

Gerald Butts, president and CEO of World Wildlife Fund Canada, has called the Coca-Cola Company "literally more important, when it comes to sustainability, than the United Nations." The reason for him is simple: raw purchasing power: "Coke is the No. 1 purchaser of aluminum on the face of the earth. . . . The No. 1 purchaser of sugar cane. The No. 3 purchaser of citrus. The second-largest purchaser of glass, and the fifth-largest purchaser of coffee."

Given this, he sees great value in joining forces with Coca-Cola. "We could spend 50 years," he goes on, "lobbying 75 national governments to change the regulatory framework for the way these commodities are grown and produced. Or these folks at Coke could make a decision that they're not going to purchase anything that isn't grown or produced in a certain way—and the whole global supply chain changes overnight. And that in a nutshell is why we're in a partnership."[17]

Even the traditionally anti-corporate organization Greenpeace has been working with Coca-Cola since 2009 on reducing greenhouse gas emissions. "Corporations," Greenpeace USA acknowledges, "can be extraordinarily dynamic, powerful, and swift allies."[18] Some activists see such cooperation as the beginning of a perilous slide toward cooptation. Still, with governments fiscally and jurisdictionally constrained and lagging badly in regulating global environmental problems, many now see partnering with big brands as one of the few ways to improve business accountability, transparency, and management. The Environmental Defense Fund's director of corporate partnerships, Gwen Ruta, justifies the EDF's partnership with McDonald's: "[T]he political system is not moving as quickly as those of us who have environmental aspirations would like—so we need to turn to the levers that we have, and one of the biggest levers is the marketplace, and in particular the clout and power that companies like McDonald's have within their own supply chain."[19]

The first partnership between a *Fortune* 500 company and environmental non-governmental organization (NGO), set up in 1990, was between the US-based Environmental Defense Fund and McDonald's to phase out styrofoam "clamshell" packaging. Some saw the move as a naive step backward. "It's like saying I'm going to join a task force with the Mafia to discuss how to cope with the drug situation," occupational health specialist Samuel Epstein reacted.[20] Such criticism did little to slow the EDF's new and seemingly effective strategy, and since then it has established many other partnerships, including one with Walmart. The EDF has even opened an office next to Walmart's headquarters in Bentonville, Arkansas. David Yarnold, the EDF's executive vice-president, explains why: "[W]hen Walmart makes important decisions, the company moves very quickly. If you are not at the table, you don't get a chance to influence those decisions. By having an office in Bentonville, we'll help to assure that the environment is represented."[21]

Today, partnerships between *Fortune* 500 companies and NGOs are common. Both big brands and NGOs have been seeking them out. Many activists recognize the irony, and even the hypocrisy, of such deals. But the desire for faster, more immediate, and more wide-ranging change is, more and more, overriding fears that these partnerships are turning environmentalism into a marketing tool. They are also providing financial support to NGOs. The WWF, for example, maintains a worldwide partnership with Coca-Cola; in 2010 worth about $20 million to the WWF. But even in these cases the reason for partnering is more to gain access to power than to receive money.

These partnerships are also of great value to big brands, legitimizing their efforts to portray themselves as sustainability champions and bolstering corporate stability and growth. Partnering with NGOs and governments, as will be discussed further in chapter 6, is enhancing the rule-making authority of big-brand companies to define sustainability—and therefore increase their influence over suppliers' practices, consumers' preferences, and government regulations. Reinforcing this authority are broader trends that, in the last few decades, have been enhancing the legitimacy and power of non-state actors to govern: such as the rise in importance of retail in the global economy, as well as privatization and deregulation. This in part explains why the global governance power of big-brand companies is rising quickly, both among corporations and in transnational governance more generally.

Are advocacy and state partners complicit in the takeover of sustainability by the big brands? The answer is surely "yes," but it is also understandable why so many groups seeking change are now partnering with these powerful players. Eco-business does seem to be both scaling up and gaining momentum. Specialized business sustainability associations are forming and strengthening. Mainstream industry associations are also increasingly adopting corporate sustainability as strategy, forming working groups on water, biodiversity, climate change, and sustainable consumption, among other things. A few industry associations are even lobbying governments for stricter environmental regulations to level the playing field, protect new comparative advantages of members, and create greater certainty.[22] As the analysis in this book reveals, however, at best the scaling up and mainstreaming of eco-business can only ever take us a short way toward genuine sustainability. And any partner should stay alert to its intrinsic limits and dangers.

The Limits of Eco-Business

Great care must be taken when evaluating the ecological or social value of eco-business. Consequences are multi-dimensional and uneven, and any gains may be temporary. Eco-business has not been, and will never be, a simple linear process of constant gains. The process will be messy and complex, with even small changes to products and processes requiring great efforts with often unanticipated setbacks. The financial investments, though measurable and real, are also a tiny fraction of a company's revenue turnover or total profits. Company forums and consortia to share sustainability ideas and cooperate on standards may even function as a veil for collusion. We saw this in 2011 with the European Commission's fine of Unilever and Procter & Gamble for price setting when introducing their "eco-friendly" line of concentrated laundry detergent (in response to Walmart's packaging demands).

Companies are achieving some eco-business targets and falling short on others. Walmart reached only half of its carbon-reduction target for 2010. Starbucks has so far failed to meet its energy-reduction and recycling targets. IKEA fell short of its 2006 commitment to reach 30 percent sustainable sourcing by 2010. Its proportion of certified chipboard and fiberboard was even further off the mark, at just 10 percent. All are promising to do better. IKEA's reason for the failure to reach its target, however, is revealing of the limits of eco-business: according to IKEA's global forestry manager, it was impossible to source sustainable wood in a way to keep prices low enough to sustain the company's rapid growth.[23]

The *total* environmental impacts of consumption, moreover, continue to increase even as the per-unit energy, material, water, and waste impacts of producing, consuming, and disposing of some consumer goods are declining.[24] The same big brands trumpeting sustainability programs are aggressively marketing "new" products to billions of "new" consumers: diapers, soft drinks, plastic razors, flip-flops, bottled water—the list could go on and on. According to Stacy Mitchell, the author of *Big-Box Swindle*, "Walmart is accelerating the cycle of consumption, speeding up how fast products move from factory to shelf to house to landfill. Even if Walmart does reduce the resources used to make a T-shirt or a television set, those gains will be more than outstripped by growth in the number of T-shirts and TVs we're consuming. It's one step forward and three steps back. . . ."[25]

Eco-business may even accelerate a decline in global environmental conditions as the same processes that are enhancing the efficiency and control of business push up consumption. The ultimate goal of eco-business is more consumption of brands and discount goods, and big brands are investing savings to expand and grow—especially in developing markets. "Sustainability is a business strategy, not a charitable giving strategy," explains Beth Keck, Walmart's senior director of sustainability. "We're thinking about sustainability from the customer's point of view. We don't want customers to have to choose between products that are sustainable or products that are affordable."[26] Absolute environmental gains are an incidental outcome rather than the goal of eco-business. It doesn't aim to curtail consumption to stop ecological loss; it helps to ensure that any loss doesn't impede more goods and more growth.

Eco-business is not about transforming the world economy that underpins today's global environmental crisis. It is about advancing the growth of ever-larger businesses. It assumes—indeed it needs—increasing production and consumption for its dynamism and rationale. Scaling back consumerism or eliminating brands or products with high social costs are not part of what eco-business is aiming to change. Consumers are the ultimate source of brand power: more consumers, buying more brands, creates more power. Eco-business cannot be divorced from lobbying efforts to lower corporate taxes. Nor is it possible to separate it from advertising efforts to convince consumers to want—and to buy—ever more stuff. The same big-brand company investing millions in sustainability is weaving brand messaging into children's TV shows, blockbuster movies, and prime-time sitcoms. And the power of brands over popular culture continues to grow, with entire films and TV dramas now made for the purpose of marketing brands. John Wells, the producer of *The West Wing*, *ER*, and *Third Watch*, lamented this in 2011: "The day isn't far off [when] brands will have more power than writers."[27]

Big-brand companies are the backbone of a world retail economy that is mass-producing cheap consumer goods designed for rapid obsolescence and turnover. Maintaining high sales for these goods relies on shifting the environmental and social costs of production and consumption onto less powerful and distant regions, ecosystems, and future generations. Some so-called gains from eco-business, such as replacing products or processes, may also cast equally, if not more damaging, ecological shadows of consumption.[28] The genius of Walmart's founder, Sam Walton, was his pursuit of ever-lower costs and ever-higher sales. His goal was more warehouse-style stores and more control of low-end markets, aiming to increase long-term total profits rather than maximize short-term profit margins. In theory, this strategy doesn't require more consumption worldwide, just more sales and market control for Walmart. Yet in practice it does tend to stimulate wasteful and excessive consumption, as options rise, as prices fall, and as more and more shoppers look, in Walmart's words, to "save money" and "live better."

Turning sustainability into eco-business, moreover, is altering the nature of environmentalism, increasing its power to accelerate some forms of change, but limiting what is on the table to question, challenge, and alter. Sustainability as an idea can be radical: not just calling for changes in the rules of the game (i.e., market dynamics), but also to the game itself (i.e., the global economy). It can, for instance, challenge individuals to reduce consumption. It can challenge businesses to stop certain practices, eliminate certain products, and produce more durable goods. And it can challenge public and private organizations to operate systems within ecological and social principles, and not just within economic ones. The big brands' takeover of sustainability, however, is shifting the purpose and goal of sustainability governance toward the need to create business value as an outcome of pursuing sustainability. And the levers of change within resulting governance mechanisms are increasingly under the control of large private organizations. States and NGOs can advance some causes by stepping strategically on these levers. But eco-business on its own cannot—and never will—alter the underlying logic of accelerating consumerism and unequal globalization behind the increasing power of big brands.

For some, this is the full story, and it signals a future with even less hope. For them, big brands will never be part of any sustainability solution. For at least some of those working on trying to implement sustainability, however, the big brands' takeover of sustainability is a still-unfolding tale that needs more actors to join for any hope of creating a more sustainable pathway forward.

A Branded World

"As businesses, we have a responsibility to society," Lee Scott Jr. asserted in January 2009 in his last public speech as Walmart's CEO. "Let me be clear about this point. There is no conflict between delivering value to shareholders, and helping solve bigger societal problems."[29]

The language of eco-business can sound self-serving and self-congratulatory. Yet it can be hard-hitting, too, looking nothing like billboard advertising. A 2011 World Economic Forum report, for example, seeing a "perfect storm" on the horizon as populations grow, natural resources decline, and climate change escalates, argues that "current pathways to sustainability do not offer the speed or scale required to meet the challenge." Looking inside the business world, the report recognizes that there are "plenty of examples of individual success stories on sustainability," yet "in aggregate, these do not add up to the change needed."[30] This might sound more like environmental advocacy than an industry report. Yet heavyweights, including Best Buy, Kraft, Nestlé, Nike, Unilever, and Walmart, sit on the Industry Partners project board for the World Economic Forum's sustainability work.

Particular corporate visions of sustainability can differ sharply. And relatively few employ the language of this World Economic Forum report. Still, the underlying message among big brands is increasingly the same. The path to corporate sustainability requires big-brand companies to participate—indeed, to lead and perhaps even brand the process. This is necessary, big brands' CEOs say, to attain the speed and scale for systemic change in a world where governments are now doing more posturing than implementing, and where civil society groups simply do not have the raw power to produce transformational global change.

Is this corporate takeover of sustainability a catastrophe for the global environmental movement? Some activists are shouting "yes" and are trying to fight back. Far more, though, are choosing to engage, partner, and give big brands some credit for changing strategies, at least for now. This is a contentious decision. Some are accusing them of selling out: of weakening a once-influential movement willing to challenge a ruinous world order. Still, it is easy to see why so many are tempted—and why some decide—to partner. Doing so seems to bring the *potential* to manage global environmental change in ways able to keep pace with the pressures from a rapidly growing and globalizing retail economy. Is this realistic? As an isolated strategy, it would seem not to be; the underlying motives and drivers of eco-business will prevent it. Yet some good can certainly come out of engaging eco-business. One aim of this book is to help reveal some of these opportunities while, along the way, dropping bright red buoys on the many dangers just below the surface.

2

The Eco-Business Setting

Why has eco-business become such a valuable and effective strategy for big-box retailers and brand manufacturers since 2005? The mainstreaming of environmentalism and the growing power of retail companies are contributing factors. But it is the combination of these factors with new risks and opportunities in the world economy, this chapter will argue, which is creating a "perfect storm" of conditions. Together they are contributing to a global business setting where pursuing corporate sustainability is of interest not only to a select few firms selling eco-products, but is also increasingly a highly efficient tool for big brands looking for ways to both project an image of responsibility while simultaneously delivering business returns. Three trends in the world economy in particular are creating incentives for companies to embrace eco-business: continuing globalization of production, with China rising fast and pathways of supply becoming longer and more complex; increasing uncertainty and instability of resource supplies and global markets; and a rapidly growing middle class across the developing world.

In this setting, eco-business is helping big brands to manage risks within supply chains, enhance brand loyalty, and reach new and emerging markets. Paradoxically, as resource scarcities and climate change intensify, it is proving ever more valuable for controlling supply chains for quality and consistency. In view of the win-win prospects for brands, the turn toward eco-business is likely to keep accelerating. Along with the continuing growth and shift of brand retail into developing countries, this trend will further concentrate global power in the hands of big-brand companies. The conclusion here is compelling: the impact of big brands on global sustainability is set to keep rising with even greater speed and intensity.

To understand why big brands now see so many advantages from using sustainability as a business tool, it is first necessary to step back to the beginning of the 1970s and trace out the steady rise, popularization, and corporatization of the global environmental movement since then.

The Rise of Global Environmentalism

On April 22, 1970, about 20 million people gathered across the United States for one of the largest organized demonstrations ever held: the first Earth Day, a "teach-in" to raise awareness of the growing plight of the world's natural environment. Around this time, more and more people were seeing footage of environmental disasters on new TVs, reading about international affairs, and communicating across cultures. The image of the earth from space was becoming a symbol of the need to think— and act—differently. Steadily, environmentalism as a movement of ideas and principles was going global, evolving into one of the most influential movements of the late twentieth century and the early twenty-first century.[1]

Global environmentalism gained increasing influence in the 1970s and the 1980s. During this period, environmental NGOs and "green" political parties formed, and states established environmental departments and signed into force domestic and international laws to regulate corporations and protect the environment. Frequent protest campaigns, marches, and demonstrations called for radical changes: bans on toxics and pollution, a halt to nuclear proliferation, wilderness and species protection, an end to whaling and sealing, reduced economic growth, and simplification of lifestyles. Newly formed international environmental organizations, among them the World Wildlife Fund/World Wide Fund for Nature (now known as simply WWF), Greenpeace, and Friends of the Earth, spearheaded the global environmentalist agenda. Governments, corporations, and consumers were the primary targets of campaigns.

During this period, corporations, primarily trying to fight back, established public-relations departments to reassure their customers and defend their reputations. By the beginning of the 1990s, however, global environmentalism was significantly influencing markets as well as the regulatory climate for investing and trading. Multinational corporations had little choice but to respond in a more cooperative manner—or, at least, in a manner that appeared to be more cooperative.[2] Public-relations and marketing departments shifted from defending the company to promoting its environmental record. The environmental activist Jay Westerveld coined the word "greenwashing" for many such efforts.[3]

Corporate Environmentalism

The 1987 report of the World Commission on Environment and Development (widely known as the Brundtland Commission) and the 1992 UN Conference on Environment and Development in Rio de Janeiro marked a turning point in global environmentalism and the regulatory approach toward corporations. Environmentalism started to broaden with the increasing acceptance of the concept of sustainable development: expanding economic growth to meet societal needs while protecting the environment for present and future generations. Corporations were urged to play a role in achieving sustainable growth and building a greener economy through proactive voluntary corporate compliance efforts.[4]

Government environmental agencies continued to regulate industry, but through softer means that emphasized market incentives and industry self-regulation. Largely out of frustration with slow state processes and with the worsening condition of the global environment, such as deforestation and climate change, environmental NGOs began working more cooperatively with multinational corporations. Traditional instruments such as international conventions and laws were still deemed necessary. Yet increasingly activists turned to multinational corporations, seeing them as more resourceful than governments and able to act faster, with a capacity to address environmental problems that crossed state borders.

Global environmentalism began to change as environmental NGOs moderated calls for radical transformation—such as reducing consumption, slowing resource usage, and limiting economic growth—and opted to pursue incremental market-driven advances instead. With a softened but more pragmatic activist position, and with governments emphasizing market-based regulatory approaches, global environmentalism moved more into the corporate realm. In doing so, it has increasingly moved from the "politics of limits" to a broader effort to "green" the economy.[5]

Since 1992, many companies have put in place environmental policies and codes of practice; many have also been actively partnering with NGOs and participating in voluntary eco-certification programs, such as those for fisheries, forestry, and organic agriculture. Today multinational corporations play a powerful role in global environmentalism, many not just responding to but also actively shaping governments, environmental groups, and consumer interests and expectations. Environmental groups know that companies still work to block, stall, and counteract environmental regulations and criticisms. Business executives continue to finance political parties and lobby politicians. They continue to deploy industry scientists to generate uncertainty. And they continue to sue governmental agencies. Especially in developing countries, multinational and local corporations also continue to fund military operations and bribe enforcement officers. Yet, for big brands anyway, an increasing priority is to guide and leverage environmentalism for growth and competitive advantages.

Global environmentalism has changed significantly since the 1960s. No longer on the political fringes, it has softened and become a global force shaping international law, state policies, business practices, and community life everywhere. People in every culture and organization—Greenpeace activists, bureaucrats at the US Environmental Protection Agency, analysts at the World Bank, employees and executives at Walmart—now describe themselves as "environmentalists." In view of its growing influence, activists, corporations, and governments continue to battle to control environmentalism. Companies are still fighting back against high-profile environmental campaigns. Yet all are also staking out territory *within* the environmental movement, embracing "corporate sustainability." The striking increase of the retail economy and the corresponding buying power of big retail chains over the last few decades have created strong incentives and new opportunities for big brands to lead these efforts.

The Growth of Big Retail

Retail is the locomotive of the world economy. It accounts for nearly one-third of world gross domestic product (GDP) (9 percent directly and 20 percent indirectly). Over the last two decades, it has become particularly important as household savings rates in the United States and Western Europe have fallen to virtually zero. Big brands have been influential forces in the retail sector, stimulating consumerism through marketing and retail chains, particularly big-box stores.[6] Consumer spending now accounts for about 70 percent of all employment and economic activity in developed economies. Worldwide, consumers in 2006 were spending at the rate of $90,000 per second, or $5.4 million per minute.[7] And this rate has been climbing annually—even with the global financial turmoil since 2007.

The rise and market concentration of brand retailers since the 1980s has been especially significant, with large chain retailers accounting for an increasing share of consumer dollars. According to the US Census of Retail Trade, until the late 1970s American consumers spent most of their money at small, family-run stores. By the end of the 1990s, however, more than 60 percent of product purchases had shifted to large retail chains. (See figure 2.1.) Rather than shopping at local lumber yards and at small hardware, appliance, and gardening stores, more than 22 million customers now visit a Home Depot outlet every week for one-stop shopping. The average Home Depot store has an area of about 130,000 square feet and stocks from 40,000 to 50,000 different products. The growth of retail chains has been remarkable. Gap Inc., characterized as "one of the retail industry's amazing success stories," increased its sales of apparel by 24,000 percent from 1984 to 1999.[8] Retail stores aren't just getting bigger; they are increasingly ubiquitous, and they are changing people's shopping habits. More than 80 percent of Americans now live within 15 miles of a Walmart store.

Retail chains are continuing to grow quickly and to concentrate, fewer companies capturing an increasing share of the consumer goods market. As of 2010, the top 250 global retailers

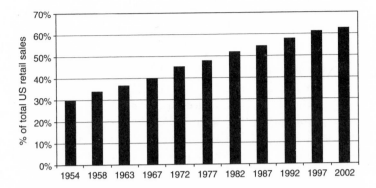

Figure 2.1
Growth of big retail sales, 1954–2002. Source: U.S. Census of Business and US Census of Retail Trade as calculated by Emek Basker and Pham Hoang Van, Putting a Smiley Face on the Dragon: Wal-Mart as Catalyst to U.S.-China Trade (working paper 07-10, University of Missouri Department of Economics, 2010), p. 31.

had combined sales of $3.9 trillion, the top 10 companies accounting for 29 percent of the sales (table 2.1).[9] Walmart alone accounted for just under 11 percent of the global 250 total.

The world's biggest general merchandise chains, among them Walmart, Carrefour, Metro, and Tesco, now reach into every part of the world, often with several different retail formats—hypermarkets, supermarkets, warehouse discount, convenience stores—under the same company roof. Carrefour, for example, operates all of these formats, with more than 9,500 stores in 33 countries, including Mexico, China, Brazil, and India.

Walmart's rise has been particularly impressive. (See figure 2.2.) Its sales revenues in fiscal year 1979 were $1 billion. Only 15 years later, its sales revenues exceeded $1 billion *per week*. And revenue growth has been accelerating since then. Total revenue in fiscal year 2005 was US$285 billion. By then Walmart had 1,500 stores. Five years later, nearly 7,000 new stores

Table 2.1
Top ten global retailers, 2010.

		Country of origin	Sales, 2010 ($ billion)	Countries of operation
1.	Walmart	United States	418.9	16
2.	Carrefour S.A.	France	119.6	33
3.	Tesco plc	UK	92.1	13
4.	Metro AG	Germany	88.9	33
5.	The Kroger Co.	United States	82.2	1
6.	Schwarz	Germany	79.1	26
7.	Costco Wholesale Corp.	United States	76.2	9
8.	The Home Depot Inc.	United States	68.0	5
9.	Walgreen Co.	United States	67.4	2
10.	Aldi	Germany	67.1	18

Source: *Switching Channels: Global Powers of Retailing 2011* (Deloitte Touche Tohmatsu, 2011), p. 11.

having opened during that period, its sales exceeded US$400 billion. In fiscal year 2010 (ending January 31, 2010), its total revenues were more than $120 billion higher than the world's second-largest and third-largest companies, the oil multinationals Royal Dutch Shell and Exxon Mobil. A year later, Walmart's total revenues were up another $17 billion or so, still $67 billion above the second-biggest company, Exxon Mobil. A year after that (FY2012), its revenues reached $443 billion.

The "Walmart Nation" now has more than 2.2 million employees.[10] If Walmart were a national economy, it would rank ahead of Sweden, Israel, Austria, and South Africa. And it is continuing to grow toward the $500 billion mark in revenues. Walmart's competitive advantage is rooted in a discount

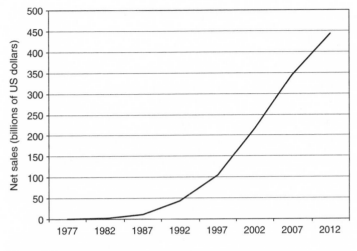

Figure 2.2
Walmart's revenues, 1977–2012. Source: Walmart annual reports.

strategy of high-volume, low-cost product sourcing. Product margins are kept low, with the goal of maintaining "unbeatable" prices in no-frills, warehouse-size retail outlets. To support its growth and its continued dominance of the market, Walmart is using advanced technology to coordinate—and generate—unsurpassed supply-chain efficiencies in the production, packaging, shipping, and distribution of hundreds of thousands of products crisscrossing the world. The US Department of Defense has even studied Walmart's highly sophisticated logistical systems to see what it might learn.

Since the 1990s, many other big-box retailers have been surging and growing, too—in many cases by using discount strategies similar to Walmart's. Thirty years ago "retail" was not even a category in the Global *Fortune* 500 list of the world's biggest companies. Today, as was noted in chapter 1, about fifty retailers are on this list. A glance at other big retailers across various "specialty" categories (such as consumer electronics, home improvement, and office supplies) shows a consistent and steady rise in sales over the past three decades. (See figure 2.3.)

Up until the 1990s, large manufacturers of packaged consumer goods—brands such as Coca-Cola, PepsiCo, Nestlé, Procter & Gamble, and Johnson & Johnson—held dominant positions within product supply chains, in part because they were more highly consolidated relative to the fragmented retail sector. This has shifted, however, as retail chains have grown in size and concentration. The manufacturing giants above and many others now count on retail chains (Tesco, Metro, Carrefour, Walmart, and others) for a sizable percentage of their sales.

Retail chains are using their buying power to influence the brand manufacturers and at times even set the terms of purchasing agreements. They are also gaining market power relative to brand manufacturers by introducing their own store-brand labels, dealing directly with producers, and cutting into

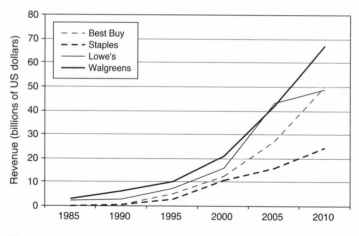

Figure 2.3
The rise of specialty retail chains, 1985–2010. Source: Company Annual Reports.

the brand manufacturer's market share by taking over some of their traditional shelf space and sales. Still, as tables 2.2 and 2.3 show, the large consumer-goods manufacturers remain powerful economic forces, maintaining a strong competitive position through name brand recognition and continual marketing innovation and selling "more variations of products in more places to more types of customers."[11]

Increasingly, too, big-brand retailers and manufacturers are cooperating to expand markets and achieve market gains together. This is particularly true for sustainability. Unilever Global, for example, explains on its website that it provides Walmart with ongoing "expert support in the areas of food and agriculture, chemical intensive products, packaging, greenhouse gas reduction initiatives and its expansion into international markets." Walmart selected Unilever as its "Best Global Supplier" in 2010. Big brands are also joining corporate-led consortia. One example is the Consumer Goods Forum in Europe. Formed in 2009 to "unite" retailers and manufacturers, it brings together more than 400 retail and manufacturing companies to collaborate on a vision of creating "better lives through better business."

Brand power is not limited to big-box general merchandisers, specialty retail chains, and consumer-goods manufacturers. All consumer sectors, including the entertainment, hospitality, food-service, communications technology, and automotive sectors, have well-established brand powerhouses: Disney, Hilton, McDonald's, Intel, Toyota, General Motors, and so on. For these companies, reputation is crucial to maintaining profitability and long-term business value. Reputation is tied to consumer trust, which is anchored in brand image. A company therefore goes to great lengths to guard its brands, which can rise and fall in value in relation to business practices as well as in response to social, political, and market dynamics. The

Table 2.2
Leading global brand manufacturers, 2010.

	Sales ($billion)	Brand examples
Foods and beverages		
Nestlé	105	Cheerios, Nescafé, Gerber, Kit Kat
Coca-Cola	35	Coca-Cola, Dasani, Minute Maid
PepsiCo	58	Frito-Lay, Quaker, Tropicana
Kraft	50	Cadbury, Maxwell House, Oreo
Household		
Procter & Gamble	79	Tide, Crest, Pampers, Gillette
Unilever	59	Sunlight, Dove, Hellmann's
Personal care		
L'Oreal	26	Garnier, Maybelline, Lancôme
Kimberly-Clark	20	Kleenex, Huggies, Cottonelle
Health		
Pfizer	68	Dentyne, BenGay, Rolaids, Trident
Johnson & Johnson	62	Band-Aid, Tylenol, Neutrogena
Bayer	46	Alka-Seltzer, One a Day, Bayer
Apparel		
Christian Dior	28	Christian Dior
Nike	19	Bauer, Lange, Daoust, Nike
Adidas	12	ArcTeryx, X-Mountain, Adidas
Electronics		
Samsung	134	Galaxy, Samsung
Hewlett-Packard	126	Hewlett-Packard
Hitachi	109	Hitachi
IBM	100	ThinkPad, Lenovo, IBM
Apple	65	Macintosh, iPod, iPhone, iPad
Nokia	56	Nokia

Sources: Company Annual Reports; *Fortune*, Annual Ranking of the World's Largest Corporations, 2011.

consultancy firm Interbrand annually calculates and ranks the value of the world's leading brands. (See table 2.3.)

A company must pass three tests to qualify as a global brand in Interbrand's ranking: it must have a presence on at least three continents, at least 30 percent of its revenue must come from outside its home country and no more than 50 percent from any single continent, and it must have a broad presence in emerging markets.[12] With new products in new markets, the companies whose brand value increased the most from 2009 to 2010 were Google (27 percent), Amazon (32 percent), and Apple (58 percent). Owing to internal governance challenges and declining sales in 2010, Blackberry's brand value tumbled, dropping off the top 100 brand value global ranking from the 54th spot in 2009.

The big brands are now effectively using eco-business to increase their brand value. As will be detailed in the next few sections, pressures and incentives arising from the globalization

Table 2.3
Top ten "best" global brands, 2011.

Rank	Brand	Value ($billion)
1	Coca-Cola	71.8
2	IBM	69.9
3	Microsoft	59.0
4	Google	55.3
5	General Electric	42.8
6	McDonald's	35.6
7	Intel	35.2
8	Apple	33.5
9	Disney	29.0
10	HP	28.4

Source: Interbrand, Best Global Brands Ranking for 2011.

of production, from increasing commodity volatility, from resource scarcities, and from new opportunities in emerging markets help to explain why eco-business efforts are accelerating.

Globalization of Production

For several decades, economic globalization has been simultaneously integrating trade and disaggregating production. It
is now hard for Americans or Europeans to find clothes, appliances, or furniture that were made in their home country.
Production has been fragmenting across the world economy as
multinational corporations outsource manufacturing and services. The emerging economies of Brazil, India, and China are
now major producers for those countries' growing domestic
markets as well as for manufacturers and retail stores in the
developed countries. Southeast Asia, South Africa, and Mexico
have also become regional economic hubs. To grow and compete, multinational corporations headquartered in the United
States and Europe have shifted their buying and their manufacturing away from home markets toward offshore outsourcing
and contract purchasing from small- and medium-size firms in
emerging and (to a lesser extent) developing economies.

This production model gives multinational corporations
more flexibility, better savings, and cheaper inputs. At the
same time, however, they forfeit some of the direct control
over production that integrated companies have traditionally
held. This explains in part why big brands have been working so hard in recent years to develop new ways to control
fragmented systems of production. China has become particularly important to these companies as a source of inexpensive
goods, and also as a rapidly growing market for higher-end
retail products, ranging from soap and diapers to phones and
automobiles.

The Rise of China

China's economic growth since the mid 1990s has reshaped the world's retail economy. In 2009, China surpassed Germany to become the world's largest exporter. It has become a transmission belt for many of the world's manufactured goods. China, for example, now accounts for more than one-third of the world's apparel exports, up from 15 percent in 1995. Almost all big-brand companies now source from China. One example is Mattel, the world's largest toy manufacturer. Mattel closed its last remaining US factory in 2002 to relocate the production of its billion-dollar brands—including Barbie, Hot Wheels, and Fisher-Price—to China. The story is similar for many other big brands.

To support this manufacturing, vast amounts of natural resources now flow into China. Timber is a vivid example. Relatively little timber was traded through China before the government banned logging in natural forests in 1998. Now, about half of the world's traded timber is going through China to supply processing factories. Boreal logs and pulp from Russia and tropical wood and pulp from Southeast Asia, the South Pacific, Africa, and South America account for most of this trade. From 30 percent to 80 percent of the timber going into China at any time can be illegal—perhaps logged in national parks in Indonesia, or smuggled from Burma to avoid taxes, or trucked from Russia by a Mafia-like organization. Manufacturers are turning this timber into packaging and pallets to box and ship electronics, apparel, food, and appliance exports; and it is becoming furniture, paper, books, and tissue for sale in stores.[13]

Overseas Chinese business is growing fast, too. As costs rise at home, Chinese firms are outsourcing to lesser-developed economies to lower labor and resource costs. They are linking into neighboring Thailand and Vietnam, and into other emerging economies, including Turkey, India, Mexico, and Brazil. This is further lengthening and fragmenting supply chains, adding to the need for multinational companies to find ways to coordinate across even more jurisdictions and among even more diverse suppliers, from large integrated corporations to small "mom-and-pop" shops.[14]

Managing Complexity

Walmart relies on more than 100,000 suppliers. These suppliers, in turn, link into a vast network of second-tier and third-tier sub-suppliers throughout the developing world. The large number and the geographic spread of suppliers give multinational corporations flexibility as well as savings on inputs and labor; but some risks also increase without the control under more direct ownership and local sourcing. Yet, as will be analyzed in detail in chapter 4, eco-business strategies are helping big brands to better gauge and govern these risks even as production fragments and as supply paths become longer and more intricate.

Globalizing supply with increased fragmentation of production is facilitating the rise of big-box retailers as supply-chain leaders and private governing authorities. Although still a challenge and usually not a first option, switching suppliers is easier for a mass merchandizing company (e.g., Walmart, Costco, or Target) that is buying lower-end products than it is for a company (e.g., Hewlett-Packard or Toyota) that requires more specialized and sophisticated components. Large retail buyers are consequently more prepared to move around in search of huge orders of cheaper or better-quality products to rotate on and off their store shelves—a capacity that gives them more power over suppliers, which in turn tends to increase as their market share grows and as the size of the supplier decreases. "It is not an accident," the supply-chain scholars Frederick Mayer and

Gary Gereffi write, "that many of the most prominent cases of private regulatory governance involve very large lead firms with more-or-less captive suppliers."[15] According to the historian Nelson Lichtenstein, the rise of Walmart and similar retailers in many ways mirrors the "merchant capitalism" of the nineteenth century, when big merchant houses in New York and in Liverpool had a great deal of control over global trade and production.[16]

Such market power doesn't mean that big brands are invulnerable to the actions of suppliers. Just the opposite: big brands are increasingly looking for ways to monitor and govern suppliers to reduce exposure to the risks associated with questionable production practices such as illegal sourcing, use of toxic additives, and chemical poisoning. Big brands' exposure to such risks is increasing. Safeway doesn't want bad food on its shelves. Toys "Я" Us doesn't want leaded paint in its toys. Disney doesn't want fiber from illegally deforested tropical forests in its children's books. The news media tend to give such events worldwide coverage. And consumers react quickly to such stories, especially when they involve health threats or risks to children.

In addition, governments are beginning to penalize companies for importing illegal components. One example is the 2008 amendment to the Lacey Act that allows American prosecutors to penalize retailers for importing into the United States a desk or a bed that contains illegal wood. For big brands, as will be discussed further in chapter 4, eco-business tools such as life-cycle assessments, audits, eco-labeling, and certification can be particularly effective ways of increasing the transparency and accountability of global suppliers and, ultimately, enhancing big brands' governance capacity to control the quality and the prices of products.

Scarcity and Instability

"We are living in a new world of risk," according to the World Economic Forum. "Globalization, shifting demographics, rapidly accelerating technological change, increased connectivity, economic uncertainty, a growing multiplicity of actors and shifting power structures combine to make operating in this world unprecedentedly complex and challenging for corporations, institutions and states alike."[17] Four factors in particular that have been causing turbulence in recent years are financial instability, fluctuations in the prices of commodities, scarcity of resources, and climate change.

In the United States alone, the subprime mortgage crisis caused $8.3 trillion in financial losses from June 2007 to November 2008.[18] Globally, markets tumbled, banks collapsed, capital seized up, and firms went bankrupt. Among other coping strategies, investors shifted money out of risky mortgage bonds into more secure holdings, such as commodities. With increased speculation in these markets, and with rising consumer demand from the emerging economies, the price level and volatility of commodities has soared. Commodity prices, which have been fluctuating for decades, are now reaching unprecedented highs. (See figure 2.4.) Defying the typical business cycle, commodities are in what some analysts are calling a "super cycle."[19] And the upward trend is expected to continue. Oil is of particular importance for the manufacturing and shipping of consumer goods, and some are predicting that in the near future the price of a barrel will hit $200 for the first time.

On top of financial and market challenges, businesses now face increasing uncertainties and impacts from climate change. The price for the global economy of climate-related natural disasters—from droughts, flooding, storms, and infestations—could reach into the trillions of dollars. "If present

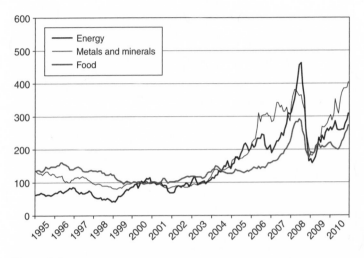

Figure 2.4
Global commodity prices, 1995–2010 (year 2000 =100). Source: World Bank data.

trends continue," a 2008 study for the Natural Resources Defense Council predicts, "the total cost of global warming will be as high as 3.6 percent of gross domestic product (GDP). Four global warming impacts alone—hurricane damage, real estate losses, energy costs, and water costs—will come with a price tag of 1.8 percent of U.S. GDP, or almost $1.9 trillion annually (in today's dollars) by 2100."[20]

A growing imbalance in the supply and demand of raw materials is presenting challenges as well. Ongoing competition and coordination problems arise because of the unequal distribution of natural resources worldwide. Rising populations in developing countries and the rapid growth of the emerging economies are increasing resource pressures and further unsettling commodity markets (sometimes shortages, sometimes surpluses). Although in 2010 China was only consuming about 10 percent as much oil per person as the United States, the

International Energy Agency is predicting that China's growing demand for oil will account for almost 60 percent of the total increase in world oil demand from 2008 to 2035. Competition for resources among industry sectors is increasing resource pressures, too. Higher demand for sugar and corn for biofuel is tightening supplies and contributing to rising food prices. The OECD-FAO *Outlook for Agriculture* projects that from 2010 to 2019 the demand for agricultural commodities will increase faster than the ability of Organization for Economic Cooperation and Development countries to supply them.

Navigating these many complexities and uncertainties is a mounting challenge. Multinational corporations must continually adjust supply chains to optimize geographic advantages and supplier performance within the context of this shifting, dynamic global marketplace. To assist, big brands are embracing eco-business governance tools: in particular, to enhance supply-chain transparency and accountability; to improve resource efficiencies and resource access; and to better anticipate and mitigate the consequences for business of growing market turbulence. Eco-business also is proving useful for reaching the growing number of middle-class consumers in developing countries.

The Emerging Middle Class

Developing states are cautiously inviting the prospects of voluntary corporate sustainability to supplement state governance capacity and development.[21] Big brands are using eco-business to gain more access to these jurisdictions and also reach the many new middle-class consumers with enough discretionary income to be able to afford higher-end consumer goods. From 2010 to 2020 another billion people are set to join this income group; 60 percent will live in emerging countries. By 2015 the number of middle-class consumers living in Asia is set to equal those in North America and Europe.[22]

The changes and prospects in these emerging economies over recent years have been dramatic. A. T. Kearney's annual Global Retail Development Index (GRDI), which assesses the top thirty developing countries for retail expansion, captures this well. From 2002 to 2011, for example, retail sales per capita in these developing countries increased on average by more than 90 percent. In particular, China, India, Russia, Vietnam, and Chile have demonstrated consistently high retail prospects on the GRDI ranking. Though lagging for a while, Brazil and Uruguay are now rising rapidly too. In 2004, Brazil wasn't even ranked on the GRDI. In 2011, it was number one, surpassing China as the most attractive retail market in the developing world (table 2.4).[23]

Every big brand is now expanding into these emerging economies—especially Brazil, China, and India—to try to capture these markets ahead of fast-growing local firms. Many are doing this under the label of "purpose-driven growth," with sustainability a central message.

Purpose-Driven Growth
The world's leading independent public-relations firm, Edelman, ranks "purpose" as the fifth "P" of marketing to compete for consumer trust and business growth: after price, product, promotion, and placement. More and more consumers in the world's fastest-growing markets (China, India, Brazil, and Mexico), according to Edelman's 2012 global survey, expect brands to support good causes, and the companies are responding.[24] Pepsi and Coca-Cola now promote their role in "hydration." Ford and General Motors are emphasizing their value for "mobility." Nokia's value proposition focuses on mobile connectivity. Nestlé emphasizes "nutrition, health, and wellness."

Table 2.4
Emerging Economy Retail Market Attractiveness Ranking, 2011.

	2011 rank	2004 rank
Brazil	1	—
Uruguay	2	—
Chile	3	12
India	4	2
Kuwait	5	—
China	6	3
Saudi Arabia	7	21
Peru	8	—
U.A.E.	9	—
Turkey	10	8
Russia	14	1
Slovenia	—	4
Croatia	—	5
Latvia	—	6
Vietnam	23	7
Slovakia	—	9

Source: A. T. Kearney, Global Retail Development Index, 2011 and 2004.

IBM's Smarter Planet initiative is positioning the company as selling "solutions" (e.g., environmental conservation and energy efficiency) rather than products.

Big-brand companies are using purpose-driven strategies to help reach and expand markets. PepsiCo, for example, is pursuing growth through "performance with purpose." Coca-Cola is looking to "energize" its brands in developing markets through its "Live Positively" sustainability program investments. Procter & Gamble now refers to its market-growth strategy as "purpose-inspired growth." The company is promoting this as an effort to "touch and improve the lives of new consumers around the world," with the goal of reaching a billion new consumers by 2015.

Branding products with purpose links corporate social responsibility to the goal of increasing sales. One component of Procter & Gamble's plan is to achieve $50 billion in sales of "sustainably driven" products by 2012. Yet Procter & Gamble's strategy also includes increasing the sales of its standard global brands. Recasting products with inherently large eco-footprints or questionable social benefits as "responsible," however, can produce irreconcilable tension and smack of hypocrisy, creating problems for the big-brand companies. They don't want consumers pondering the social and environmental value of sugary soft drinks, artificially flavored ice cream, high-fat snack foods, and bottled water. They also don't want new shoppers questioning the water-pollution and waste impacts of newly introduced products such as toilet bowl cleaners and disposable diapers.

To avoid backlash and develop new markets, companies are employing carefully crafted sustainability messaging, very broadly construed. Procter & Gamble, for example, is marketing Pampers diapers in China by emphasizing their value for providing a baby with "golden sleep." A decade ago, few parents in China had ever used a disposable plastic or paper diaper. After identifying sleep benefits as a way to build demand among mothers, in 2007 Procter & Gamble launched an advertising campaign claiming that babies in disposable diapers were falling asleep 30 percent faster and experiencing 30–50 percent less sleep disruption. The campaign included encouraging new mothers to upload pictures of their sleeping babies to the Pampers' Chinese website. The visual confirmation of the sleep value of Pampers set a Guinness World Record for the largest photomontage. The campaign has been a striking success for Procter & Gamble, and Pampers is now the best-selling diaper in China.

Some see great hypocrisy here. To counter this, some CEOs are adopting and parroting back the language and concerns of more critical environmentalists, emphasizing ideas such as "sustainable consumption" as a way to green economies and improve everyday life in countries with weak regulations and poor enforcement. One example is Unilever. Since 2010, Unilever's "Sustainable Living Plan" has been emphasizing the win-win prospects for society and the company of reaching more consumers with "environmentally responsible" and "beneficial" products such as Fair & Lovely soap and Sunlight detergent. Already, more than half of Unilever's sales are in developing countries. Unilever also argues this is a way to promote "sustainable growth." Unilever's CEO, Paul Polman, sees no conflict between Unilever being able to achieve sustainability and grow its business:

[W]e are already finding that tackling sustainability challenges provides new opportunities for sustainable growth: it creates preference for our brands, builds business with our retail customers, drives our innovation, grows our markets and, in many cases, generates cost savings . . . while ensuring that our growth does not come at the expense of the world's diminishing natural resources.[25]

Competing for the World's Eco-Business

Environmentalism has been one of the most influential and truly global movements of the last half-century. The deepening and mainstreaming of environmental organizations and regulations, both public and private, is a testimony to its reach. Differences in views of the causes of change and the best solutions exist across organizations and cultures. Yet few would dispute that citizens worldwide are more aware of pollution, species extinction, and climate change than they were in the past. Eco-markets are increasing. Activism is broadening across a range of perspectives, forums, and approaches. And states and international organizations are continuing to strengthen environmental regulations. Yet although the prevalence of environmentalism is increasing, the nature of environmentalism is changing and softening. Particularly with the rise of corporate environmentalism, the environmental movement is becoming less about radical transformation and more about incremental market improvements. This gradual corporatization of environmentalism has set the stage for the uptake of eco-business by big brands as well as the receptivity of states and NGOs to these efforts. Eco-business is building upon, extending, and deepening a process that started decades ago.

This explains in part why big-brand stores are now rushing to extend eco-business—a trend that a shifting and rising world retail economy is reinforcing. Yet this is only a partial reason for big-brand companies accelerating adoption of eco-business. To enhance performance and stay competitive in today's macroeconomic conditions, big brands increasingly need to find efficiencies, enhance brand loyalty, expand into emerging markets, navigate financial turmoil and price shocks, and manage long supply chains for quality and consistency as resource scarcities grow. In this context, as will be documented in the next three chapters, big-brand companies are increasingly using eco-business to achieve competitive advantages.

3

The Eco-Business Market Advantage

Marks & Spencer claims it is now well on its way to becoming the world's most sustainable retailer, having already met more than half of its 180 targets, including reducing its energy and water usage, carbon emissions, packaging, chemicals, and waste per unit of production. These claims are front and center in its public relations, but Marks & Spencer also reported savings of more than $110 million in 2011 from corporate sustainability initiatives, up 50 percent from the previous year. Although the gains are small relative to overall profits, Marks & Spencer expects the returns to continue to increase. Big-brand companies across all sectors are pursuing similar eco-business prospects, and in a remarkable number of instances these prospects seem to be getting better. Going beyond corporate environmental improvements, eco-business is pursuing market advantage. The World Business Council for Sustainable Development predicts that sustainable business opportunities will be worth more than $6 trillion over the next 40 years.[1]

For some time, Interface Carpets, Ben & Jerry's, Whole Foods, Xerox, and 3M have been "poster children" for sustainability efforts. It is difficult to find a report, article, or book on corporate sustainability initiatives published in the last 20 years that doesn't include a profile and analysis of the eco-efficiency efforts of at least one of them. In view of this, some may be thinking that the rise of big-brand eco-business is "nothing new." In certain respects this is true. Some of what is now occurring is indeed a surge in longstanding eco-efficiency initiatives. Yet looking more broadly reveals a significant and worldwide shift in corporate strategy: a move toward capturing an eco-business advantage not only to improve efficiencies, but also to increase revenues and to gain advantage over competitors. This chapter documents (in many instances intentionally in the company's own language) how big-brand companies are increasingly taking command of sustainability and adopting and defining it in eco-business terms to achieve competitive advantages in their own operations.

Bottom-Line Eco-Efficiency

In 1996, Stephan Schmidheiny, the founder of the World Business Council for Sustainable Development, made an astute prediction: "within a decade it is going to be next to impossible for a business to be competitive without also being 'eco-efficient'—adding more value to a good or service while using fewer resources and releasing less pollution."[2] Since 2005, corporate programs to "produce more with less" have expanded, and efforts to integrate corporate environmental programming into the mainstream have expanded quickly.

Many factors are behind this trend. Worldwide, firms are looking for new ways to lower costs so as to stay competitive in a volatile global economy. For big-brand companies, the drive for efficiency has intensified with the need to compete in markets dominated by high-volume, low-price buyers such as Walmart. By reducing waste and lowering the energy and input costs of each unit of production, eco-efficiency can generate savings and productivity to help keep prices low. Rather than a linear flow of resources from "cradle" (extraction) to "grave" (disposal), in theory eco-efficiency allows firms to reuse and recycle materials and products through circular closed-loop processes (cradle to cradle). Companies have pitched eco-efficiency, or what some now call "eco-effectiveness," as a win-win strategy to minimize the environmental impact of each unit of production and maximize overall profit and growth potential.[3]

In comparison with some sustainability programs, the payback period from eco-efficiency programs can be short. The return on investment can therefore be easier to demonstrate, as more and more businesses are finding. FedEx, for example, recovered the capital investment from installing energy-efficient lighting at all of its Kinko's stores in just 12–18 months. In this sense, eco-efficiency is simply part of innovation and new technology adoption and has always been important in the creation of business value in high-performing companies. Xerox has realized continuous eco-efficiency gains since launching a resource recovery program in 1967 and introducing energy-saving copiers in 1969. 3M's Pollution Prevention Pays (3P) program, created in 1975, also continues to find innovative ways to lower the company's operating costs by reducing waste at source. To date, 3M estimates that the 3P program has cut more than 3 billion pounds of pollution and saved the company about $1.4 billion.[4] Eco-efficiency has been a major factor in the longevity of both companies.

Eco-business programs focused on efficiency can be grouped into four areas: conserving energy and managing carbon, reducing and recycling materials and packaging, minimizing water use, and reducing toxics and waste. (See figure 3.1.) Increasingly for big-brand companies, these are no longer small, one-off programs; instead, they are integrated company-wide to deliver tangible returns and long-term business earnings.

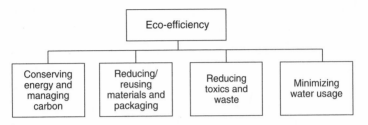

Figure 3.1
Big brands' eco-efficiency initiatives.

Energy and Carbon

Often a company's initial eco-business efforts are directed toward conserving energy, as cost savings can be quickly realized from even basic upgrades to things like lighting, air conditioning, and office equipment. Even a minor change can generate recurring savings for a multinational company. Walmart reportedly saved $1 million a year by simply removing light bulbs from its soft drink machines for employees. Yahoo reduced the cost of air conditioning its buildings by two-thirds by opening some doors and recycling cool air from the outside.[5]

Big brands' efforts to reduce energy use, however, are now moving beyond just "picking the low-hanging fruit" of business opportunities. New policies and regulations, the threat of peak oil, fluctuating oil and gas prices, and the risks of climate change are encouraging moves toward greater efficiencies and product innovation, and are spurring some companies to implement broader energy-reduction and carbon-management programs. Some companies also now see carbon-management and energy-management strategies as essential to long-run competitive positioning. More than 550 institutional investors, with assets of more than US$70 trillion, have signed on to the Carbon Disclosure Project, for example. The main reason is straightforward: investors recognize that information about the energy and carbon profiles of global companies is essential for assessing commercial risks and benefits—and thus, for financing decisions. Effective management of energy consumption and greenhouse-gas emissions has the potential to generate financial returns that send positive signals to investors. Johnson & Johnson, for example, reported a 19 percent internal rate of return on $187 million worth of capital investments in corporate-wide energy-reduction projects between 2005 and 2009.[6]

Examples now abound of companies in all industries rolling out programs to improve their bottom lines through energy-efficiency and carbon-management investments. Online e-news groups such as CSRwire, Environmental Leader, sustainable-business.com, and greenbiz.com provide daily updates on these eco-business initiatives. In consumer goods, some efforts are even spanning the product life cycle, from design, through manufacturing, distribution, sale, and use, to disposal. Procter & Gamble, Energizer Battery, Sony, Philips, and Motorola are also going beyond niche eco-markets to redesign some of their mainstream products; some of the designs are for such things as energy-efficient electric razors, solar-powered flashlights, wind-up radios, and solar-powered mobile phones. These firms are marketing some of these products (e.g., cold-water detergent) as "new" and energy conserving. Some are finding value from infusing a well-established brand with even very small sustainability changes. Hasbro announced in 2011 that it would redesign its Easy-Bake toy oven, replacing the 100-watt light bulb with a more energy-conserving heat source. Len Sauers, Procter & Gamble's vice president of global sustainability, explains the logic of such decisions as wanting to make "a meaningful improvement targeted at mainstream consumers."[7] Fundamentally though, big-brand companies are pursuing the potential of eco-business.

Hewlett-Packard, Dell, Microsoft, Intel, Apple, Samsung, Nokia, IBM, Canon, and other companies in the information and communications technology (ICT) sector are particularly focused on energy efficiency, redesigning laptops, printers, e-readers, smart phones, digital cameras, and high-definition TVs to save energy *and* money. Manufacturing a single personal computer releases about 275 kilograms of carbon dioxide and requires about 3,000 kilowatt-hours of power, an amount roughly equal to an average American family's total annual energy consumption. And depending on the usage pattern, consumer electricity costs can also add up. For market reasons, these companies are now competing to lower the power needs of a wide range of products. They are seeking ENERGY STAR and EPEAT (electronic product environmental assessment tool) approval, and marketing the "green" low-power features as performance features. Apple promotes the fast processing speed of its MacBook Pro laptop *and* claims that it has innovative energy-efficient hardware and software components with this "tag line": "Designed to make an impact. Just not on the environment."

The big ICT brands are also investing billions of dollars to improve the efficiency of their energy-intensive facilities. Cloud computing (large-scale sharing of information-technology infrastructure over the Internet) is helping to optimize computing resources, with smart meters and smart-grid systems used to monitor, track, and reduce energy consumption and costs. IBM estimates that its Intelligent Building Management software will reduce maintenance costs 10–30 percent and buildings' energy use by as much as 40 percent. ICT companies are scaling up their efforts by selling these intelligent systems to governments as well as to manufacturers of electronic household appliances. Whirlpool, the world's largest manufacturer of home appliances, is now working to make its washers, dryers, stoves, refrigerators, microwaves, and dishwashers smart-grid compatible by 2015.

Data-processing centers are a particularly important area where ICT companies are accelerating eco-business initiatives. Often housing thousands of computer servers covering an area the size of several football fields, these consume massive amounts of electricity (in computer power and cooling systems) and contribute significantly to greenhouse-gas emissions. The US Environmental Protection Agency estimates that servers and data centers—what some call "server farms"—account for as much as 1.5 percent of the United States' total electricity consumption.[8] With smart meters and better air-cooling methods, big-brand companies are pursuing ways to improve the power use effectiveness of these facilities to create large cost savings. The overall business gains are potentially very large. The Electric Power Research Institute estimates that the smart-grid market alone will be worth $1.3 trillion to $2 trillion over the next 20 years (upward of 2.5 percent of the annual $4 trillion US retail industry).[9]

Across all sectors, big brands are working to reduce energy costs. Big-box retailers are looking to implement energy-efficiency programs to try to lower the operating expenses of their retail outlets and distribution facilities (as well as counter the negative perception of big-box stores). Many are participating in the Leadership in Energy and Environmental Design (LEED) green building program for retail and the special "volume program" for high-volume property developers. As of 2008, Best Buy has been committed to building only LEED-certified stores. Among many new features, the retrofitted retail spaces include LED (light-emitting diode) lights, integrated smart-grid meters, and alternative heating sources.

Buildings alone account for about 40 percent of total energy use in the United States (and 40 percent of the world's raw materials).[10] Improving the energy efficiency of a building can produce significant savings. The ENERGY STAR program estimates that reducing a building's energy costs by 10 percent is equal to a 1.26 percent increase in sales for an average store. Big brands are finding that even tiny changes can be worthwhile financially. Among a growing number of similar eco-business examples, Walmart, by reducing its store lighting from 32 to 25 watts, reports that on average it is saving about $20,000 a year at each store. With more than 10,000 Walmart outlets worldwide, that adds up. IKEA claims that it has halved the electricity costs at its distribution center in Tejon, China by simply installing motion detectors for lighting.

Big-brand companies are also beginning to invest and experiment in renewable energy alternatives such as solar, wind, and geothermal. Toys "Я" Us is planning to save more than $300,000 a year for at least 20 years by installing the world's second-largest rooftop solar panel system at its distribution center in Flanders, New Jersey. IKEA is installing solar panels and wind turbines to help meet the electricity needs of its European stores. So far, IKEA claims that it is meeting half of its needs through wind and solar power, on its way to 100 percent reliance on renewable energy. Peter Agnefjaell, head of IKEA Sweden, explains the business benefits: "It gives us the possibility to transfer the financial benefit of electricity from our own wind power park to lower prices which will benefit our customers."[11]

Shifting to renewable energy leaves these large retail facilities far from a "sustainable operation." Nonetheless, their adoption of "green energy" measures can potentially help to scale up new, more environmentally responsible technologies, introduce these innovations to wider markets, and demonstrate the commercial value of eco-efficiency. Most important to the retailers, however, such eco-business efforts are helping to strengthen their bottom line and market position.

Big-brand companies are also increasingly looking for ways to reduce their consumption of fossil fuels and to capture cost savings within their expanding transportation and distribution systems. Faced with rising energy inputs and potential penalties from carbon emissions, big brands are seeking eco-business gains by optimizing routes, improving packing to reduce unused freight space, and putting more electric and hybrid vehicles on the road. In 2005, Walmart committed $500 million a year to improve the fuel efficiency of its US fleet of more than 7,000 trucks: the goal was a 100 percent increase in efficiency within 10 years and expected net savings of about $500 million a year by 2020. The company was reporting in 2011 that it was making strong progress toward its goal of achieving a 65 percent efficiency increase in its US fleet (from a 2005 baseline).[12]

Other companies are aiming to improve the energy efficiency of their commercial fleets, too, with many expecting future rather than immediate financial returns. There is no instant return on investment, Dennis Beal of FedEx explains. "Right now," he says, "it's strictly an investment in technology."[13] Some companies are therefore lagging. With the fourth-biggest commercial fleet in the United States, as of 2011 FedEx had converted just 2 percent of its vehicles to alternative fuels. Despite a promise made in 2010 to switch to an all-electric fleet, FedEx's main competitor, UPS, is similarly behind. But as of 2011 Best Buy had converted 52 percent of its fleet to "flexible-fuel" vehicles (able to run on gasoline blends, including ethanol). That same year, Johnson & Johnson had 1,969 hybrid vehicles on the road (25 percent of its fleet).[14] Johnson & Johnson also was investing in new green infrastructure, such as charging stations for electric vehicles.

Big-brand companies anticipate that the rising costs of fossil fuels and other factors (including cheaper batteries for hybrid vehicles) will help to generate greater future returns and usage. Coca-Cola, for example, reports that hybrid vehicles now cost about 40 percent more than standard ones, but CEO John Brock sees them as eventually paying for themselves by reducing both fuel use and emissions by 35 percent. PepsiCo is also looking to capture future eco-business gain, by converting 1,700 of its 26,000 vehicles in the United States (6 percent) to hybrid, natural gas, or hydrogen power by 2010. PepsiCo estimates the electric trucks will emit 75 percent less greenhouse gases and will generate savings of $50,000 over the lifetime of each truck.[15]

Water Efficiency

Coca-Cola proudly reports that every day its consumers drink 1.7 billion servings of its more than 500 beverage brands. As with all food and drinks, the production of Coca-Cola's products relies on vast quantities of potable water—a resource that is in increasingly short supply in many places. Making computer components also requires large amounts of clean water. To produce silicon chips, Intel and Texas Instruments used 11 billion gallons of water in 2007, equal to the capacity of about 17,000 Olympic-size swimming pools.[16]

Similar to carbon management, water management is not just an environmental issue, but also a business concern when considering future operational costs. Without mitigating action, meeting future global water demand will require infrastructure investments of as much as $200 billion a year between 2010 and 2030.[17] The markets have taken notice. More than 350 investors, with assets of US$43 trillion, have recently joined the Water Disclosure Project to increase corporate transparency on the financial costs of water-management risks.

The escalating water crisis has turned a spotlight on manufacturers in all sectors. Global water consumption has tripled over the last half-century, and by 2030 the demand is expected to exceed the supply by 40 percent. Climate change and pollution are also threatening available fresh water. Globally, on average, it takes roughly 80 liters of water to produce one dollar of industrial output. A ton of steel, for example, takes about 234,000 liters of water to produce, and an average car requires about 147,000 liters. Around 70 percent of global water usage is in agriculture, though. It takes about 75 liters of water to produce a glass of beer, 120 liters for a glass of wine, 140 liters for a cup of coffee, 1,300 liters to grow a kilogram of barley, 2,700 liters for a cotton T-shirt, and 15,500 liters to produce a kilogram of beef. Coca-Cola's daily water usage alone equals what a typical American city of 1.5 million people uses in a day.[18]

Water as a commodity is generally priced very low. Corporate water costs can be high, however, as a result of electricity needs, filtration, and chemical treatment. Water efficiency is therefore good eco-business. IBM was able to reduce its water bill by $740,000 a year by implementing "Smart Water" efficiency systems at its plant in Burlington, Vermont. Less water consumption has also saved IBM $600,000 a year in chemical and filtration costs, and $2.3 million a year in energy costs.[19] Recognizing the need to secure supplies and achieve greater water efficiency, Coca-Cola, PepsiCo, and Nestlé have been extending water goals, including claiming to aspire to one day become "water neutral" (which they define as putting as much water back into the global system as they are taking out).

A community that had seen its local wells run dry by a multinational corporation would be justified in challenging the plausibility of these commitments, and no big brand is even close to becoming water neutral. The promised environmental benefits are debatable, too. Efficient water use doesn't mean less total use—just less use per unit of production. Slowing total production and consumption is not part of the equation. And although a company may claim "water neutrality" as calculated on a balance sheet, the environment may be no better off. Severe ecological impacts can arise from diverting and "replacing" water. Still, at least to a limited extent, big-brand companies are improving some of their water-management practices—for example, by implementing treatment systems to decrease water withdrawals and reduce costs, aiming to return wastewater to the watershed in at least as good a state as when it was withdrawn. (See chapter 5.) Levi Strauss's new water policy requires its manufacturers to "clean" any water used before returning it to the environment.

Eco-business goals of enhancing resource security and cost efficiency are encouraging these efforts. Improving water efficiency means that there is less water to pump, less to treat, and less to dispose of per unit of product produced. Coca-Cola's CEO, Muhtar Kent, explains: "We've put a stake in the ground with our commitment to water neutrality. This is good for business because it lowers our cost of production, it lowers our break-even points, and it allows us to spend more money on our brands."[20] Nestlé's chairman, Peter Brabeck-Letmathe, is frank: unless the world can solve the worsening water crisis, his 150-year-old company won't make it to the 200-year mark.[21]

Materials and Packaging

Eco-business efforts to improve the efficiency of material use go hand in hand with an effort to save on energy and water costs. This includes reducing the input of materials that go into each product as well as using better or more appropriate materials to improve recyclability and reduce toxicity. As with energy efficiency, companies have been pursuing these efforts for many decades with many successful results. A pound of aluminum, for example, can now generate 60 percent more cans than it did 35 years ago.[22] Big-brand companies are now seeking further eco-business gains to keep input costs down and production volumes up.

For IKEA, the world's biggest home-furnishings company, cutting back on materials and packaging to lower costs is essential for competitiveness. IKEA furniture is designed to optimize the use of materials to keep prices low. This dates back to 1956, when IKEA first "flat-packed" its Lövet table by taking off the legs so more tables would fit into a shipping container. Today, the company reports that it is concentrating even more on what it calls "smart packaging" to further reduce package size and save money on materials and freight. IKEA explains that its goal is to phase out its solid-wood usage by substituting redesigned materials, such as "board-on-frame" that sandwiches stiff cardboard between thin sheets of wood veneer or cardboard shipping crates to replace traditional wooden crates. The eco-business strategy is straightforward: to reduce dependence on natural timber to reduce risks and save money.

Again, even a tiny change in material efficiency can generate financial gains and decrease a product's environmental footprint. Yet, as before, the real motivation here is business value. General Mills' decision to flatten its Hamburger Helper noodles cut the use of 900,000 pounds of paper per year, reduced its carbon emissions by 11 percent, and took 500 trucks off the road. At the same time, General Mills was able to put 20 percent more of the now-smaller packages onto the same Walmart shelves, increasing sales potential.[23]

"Lightweighting" strategies to downsize packaging through redesign, material reduction, and increasing recycled content are gaining even greater business importance with rising commodity prices, growing concerns over greenhouse-gas emissions, the increasing cost of freight, and new packaging laws. Some big brands are also using "downsizing" as a strategy to disguise price increases—marketing smaller packages with less product inside as "greener," thus increasing profit margins. Many are going further, though. Nike explains that it is drawing on a philosophy of "keep it light" that the company's co-founders, Bill Bowerman and Phil Knight, developed while coaching and running track at the University of Oregon. One of Nike's business goals is to "eliminate what's not critical": to leverage eco-business to improve performance, efficiency, and profit margins.

Corrugated cardboard is one of Nike's largest material purchases. And the shoebox and its shipping carton constitute much of the company's packaging costs. Nike has designed a new, lighter box that is claimed to require 30 percent less material than its 1995 box, and is 100 percent recyclable. The company estimates this will save almost 12,000 metric tons of cardboard annually—equal to about 200,000 trees—as well as improve the company's bottom line. Nike is not alone here. Its competitor Brooks redesigned its shoebox to use less material, and also stopped stuffing tissue paper in the toes of new shoes and putting moisture-absorbing silica bags in shoe boxes. Brooks estimates that these changes reduced the cost of their shoeboxes by 38 percent. Puma, another maker of athletic shoes, replaced its shoeboxes with reusable bags.

Many other companies are pursuing and reporting similar savings through eco-business. Coca-Cola claims to have saved more than $100 million in 2009 by reducing its packaging by 85,000 metric tons. An early example of how Coca-Cola began achieving these savings is the "Ultra Glass" bottle. Introduced in 2000, it is 20 percent lighter and 10 percent cheaper than the conventional bottle. Since then Coca-Cola claims to have found even more ways to reduce material inputs: for example, reducing plastic use by about 5 percent by shortening the height of the closure at the top of the bottle to allow for smaller bottle caps. Coca-Cola claims that this minor adjustment cut its plastic purchases by about 40 million pounds a year in the United States alone.

Soft drink companies face an especially difficult sustainability image challenge. Billions of branded drink containers continue to end up as litter in parks and roadsides, or to be dumped into landfills. To try to counter this, Coca-Cola is adopting eco-business to try to change perceptions of its packaging. Coca-Cola's long-run aim is to make plastic bottles from 100 percent renewable materials. Although not compostable, they will (like their other containers) be technically recyclable. In November 2009, Coca-Cola announced the global rollout of a new 100 percent recyclable polyethylene terephthalate (PET) bio-plastic PlantBottle made from up to 30 percent plant materials (e.g., sugarcane ethanol from Brazil). Muhtar Kent explains: "Right now we're investing in the PlantBottle, and we know it's going to cost a little more than virgin resin materials in the beginning. But every indication is that it's going to cost significantly less as we move forward and it scales up. And it's going to be great for the planet also, because we're using less petroleum, a finite resource."[24]

Much as there are concerns and uncertainties about the aggregate ecological impacts of other eco-business initiatives, there is much debate about the actual net environmental impact of the PlantBottle, particularly regarding the ecological consequences of the plant material sourcing. Nevertheless, big-brand companies are moving ahead quickly. Heinz has partnered with Coca-Cola to convert its ketchup bottle to plant material. And in 2011, PepsiCo developed the world's first 100 percent plant-based plastic PET bottle, made from switch grass, pine bark, and corn husks. The company "piloted" the bottle in 2012 with the stated aim of full-scale commercialization.

Technology companies, meanwhile, are redesigning their packaging to reduce volume, increase recycled content, and increase curbside recyclability. Dell is taking what it calls the "Three C approach," the three C's being Cube, Content, and Curb. The Cube aspect asks "How big is the box? Could it be smaller?" The Content aspect asks "What is the packaging made of? Could it be made of something better?" The Curb aspect asks "Is it easily recycled?" Dell is now striving to use bamboo packaging to protect its notebook computers instead of using plastic cushioning; the bamboo is compostable and is sourced from certified plantations in China. As with the plant bottle, the net environmental impacts of non-recyclable bamboo versus traditional recyclable post-consumer content corrugated cardboard are unclear, but for Dell the outcomes are clear— the company is reporting that the eco-business initiative has attracted positive customer attention and has lowered costs.

Procter & Gamble plans to reduce the costs of packaging its shampoos and beauty products by making plastic containers from sugarcane-derived ethanol from Brazil. Procter & Gamble and Unilever have also halved the overall size of their liquid laundry detergent packaging. According to the companies, this has saved materials (e.g., plastic), resources (e.g., water), and shipping space, all of which translates into energy savings during manufacturing and transportation.

Walmart's decision to sell only concentrated detergent in its American stores after May 2008 spurred Procter & Gamble's and Unilever's moves. Walmart sells about one-fourth of all the liquid laundry detergent sold in the United States. Its decision to only sell concentrated detergent, Walmart claims, is saving more than 400 million gallons of water, 95 million pounds of plastic resin, and 125 million pounds of cardboard every year. Since 2008, Walmart has introduced a packaging scorecard to evaluate material efficiency to get at further savings. To support this, it has declared that suppliers must use sustainable packaging to retain access to its store shelves, a decision that is increasing the productivity of suppliers, the efficiency of supply, and the financial gains for the big brands.

Still, big brands have many unrealized opportunities to pursue eco-business advantages. Much of what ends up in landfill is packaging. "We're burning and landfilling 40 million tons of recyclable packaging materials estimated to be worth $15 to $23 billion every year," Conrad MacKerron of the advocacy group As You Sow explained in a shareholder resolution statement to both Procter & Gamble and General Mills in April 2011 calling for greater extended producer responsibility.[25] Big brands are taking heed, however, and using eco-business to increase the competitive opportunity from turning waste into profit.

Waste and Toxics

Eco-business is linking energy-efficiency and material-efficiency initiatives with efforts to reduce waste and some toxics—with, again, an eye on lowering costs and finding profits. Companies that are leading here are analyzing and assessing the hazards and recyclability of materials to try to reuse more and discard less. Motivated by an aspirational goal of "zero landfill," employees at Subaru's Indiana plant literally take the challenge into their own hands by "dumpster diving"—inspecting and analyzing the company's trash to think up new ideas for reducing, reusing, or recycling. Waste adds unnecessary costs for treatment or disposal without adding any product value, and in this sense trying to run a lean operation has always made good business sense. "Waste is cost to the corporation" explains Johnson & Johnson's senior director of Worldwide Health and Safety Al Iannuzzi, ". . . and, of course, the less waste you send out of your gates, the less expensive it is to make your product."[26] Again, some of these eco-business efforts involve tiny changes that produce recurring savings. Walmart, for example, reports that it is now earning millions a year by collecting loose plastic (which in the past was discarded) and selling it back to manufacturers.

Toyota set the stage in the 1980s with a lean manufacturing model meant to get rid of defects, production downtime, and excess inventory. Many big-brand companies have been relying on the philosophy of lean manufacturing to reduce waste. Now, however, as was discussed in chapter 2, efforts are accelerating to lower the costs of waste disposal and reduce the need for raw material inputs. Again, most efforts tend to be small, although together these small efforts can add up to create eco-business advantages, both financial and reputational, for big-brand companies. IKEA has removed plastic bags from its stores in Australia, the UK, and the US, as have a growing number of other retailers. Hewlett-Packard is accepting back used print cartridges. Sony, in its new Vaio laptops, has replaced almost one-fourth of the non-recycled content with recycled CDs.

Some waste-reduction efforts are extending. Dell now offers free recycling of all computer equipment regardless of the manufacturer and is two-thirds of the way to meeting its goal of a billion pounds of diverted e-waste by 2014. Best Buy also provides free recycling through its "greener tomorrow" campaign, aiming by 2015 to collect a billion pounds of used consumer electronics ("e-waste") to be refurbished, resold, or recycled.

In pursuing eco-business advantages, some companies are also looking to improve the recyclability of brand products by more carefully vetting design, including reducing and eliminating some toxic components. Using a life-cycle approach, Nike has developed a tool it calls the "Considered Index" to evaluate the potential environmental impacts of new products (e.g., solvent use, waste, materials, and treatments) before they are commercialized. Since 2009, Walmart has also been more closely assessing products for toxics, using its GreenWERCs tool to screen chemical-based products for any chemicals of concern. Such tools are designed to help protect consumers but also corporate growth as the number of "new and improved" products adding new chemicals with unknown health and environmental consequences continues to grow daily. A 2011 study by the University of California at Berkeley in cooperation with the Nicholas School of Environment at Duke University found that 80 percent of the 101 polyurethane foam baby products sampled (e.g., changing pads, nursing pillows, crib mattresses, car seats) contained toxic or untested halogenated flame retardants and 36 percent contained a banned carcinogenic substance known as chlorinated tris.[27]

At the same time, though, big-brand companies have made some progress toward reducing some toxics. Procter & Gamble has eliminated polyvinylchloride (PVC) from most of its "clamshell" and "blister" packages. Mattel no longer sells vinyl plastic PVC toys. Estée Lauder, L'Oréal, and SC Johnson are working with suppliers to remove phthalates (hormone-disruptive substances that help fragrances last longer). Computer and technology companies, meanwhile, are making progress toward promises to phase out chemicals like PVC and brominated flame retardants (BFR) from computers and to eliminate mercury from the screens of notebook computers. In 2010, IBM met its commitment to eliminate perfluorooctane sulfonate (PFOS) and perfluorooctanoic acid (PFOA) from its microprocessor chip manufacturing process—substances used as stain or water repellents in many consumer products. Big-brand companies are realizing business value from their efforts in terms of improved product quality, risk management, and consumer trust. Praise from activist watchdogs (e.g., the Greenpeace annual review and ranking of the "greenest" technology companies) is reinforcing these business gains.

Companies, particularly manufacturers of household products, are also seeing eco-business value in what they call the "green chemistry" of some of their products. SC Johnson is investing in a "Greenlist" process that claims to encourage safer raw materials, and it now has a "What's Inside" website that lists the ingredients of various products. Clorox has followed suit, introducing a website to inform consumers and launching an "Ingredients Inside" program in North America to display ingredients on product labels.

More and more big-brand companies, then, are seeing eco-business as a way of improving efficiency, resource productivity, and profit margins as well as a way to stimulate innovation, increase quality, and enhance competitiveness. Nike's popular Trash Talk basketball shoe, for example, costs less, supposedly looks cool, performs well, and is made entirely from waste from the factory floor. All of this is certainly good for public relations and brand reputation; and it is also helping Nike to develop new markets and increase sales. Trash Talk shoes sold out within hours of going on sale in 2008, and won "best in show" at the 2009 International Design Show.

Top-Line Growth

Eco-business will become more expensive and its targets more difficult to reach as big-brand companies move past the relatively easy gains from eco-efficiency. Yet eco-business is not simply spurred by the need for more bottom-line efficiency. Big brands are also integrating eco-business targets and tools to attract new customers, increase sales, and enter emerging markets. Brands compete within product categories around innovation, quality, and price. They also compete around brand recognition, marketing, and consumer loyalty. Eco-business is an increasingly effective lever to help meet these competitive priorities in the face of maturing markets and recessionary pressures. "Companies with a commitment to sustainability," A. T. Kearney found in a market study covering the 2007–2009 global financial downturn, "outperformed their peers during the financial crisis by 15%."[28] One source of value is coming from mainstreaming eco-markets.

Scaling Up Eco-Markets

Eco-markets still make up only a small share of the total market. Typically, though, these are growing at double the rate of traditional ones.[29] They are also expanding as companies introduce mainstream brands to these markets. By 2008, American consumers were spending close to $300 billion on products like organic foods, natural cleansers, and energy-efficient appliances—up more than 30 percent from 2005. And the competitive opportunities from eco-products continue to rise. Eco-product sales at Kingfisher, Europe's leading home-improvement retailer, roughly doubled in the period 2008–2012 (to £1.4 billion, and to about 13 percent of total sales). McGraw-Hill Construction is projecting that the American market for green buildings will increase 170 percent from $50 billion in 2010 to $135 billion by 2015. And four years after launching Ecomagination in 2005, General Electric was already reporting $17 billion a year in revenue from its greener products and technologies. The company is predicting these revenues will grow at twice the rate of total corporate revenue over the next few years. Procter & Gamble, too, was already reporting by 2007 that its green design products were generating about $10 billion a year in sales (12 percent of the company's sales), and expected sales of such products to reach $20 billion by 2012.[30]

Big brands have recognized the growth opportunity from producing and marketing eco-products. For one, they are buying up "ethical brands." Unilever purchased Ben & Jerry's in 2000. Clorox purchased Burt's Bees in 2007. Colgate Palmolive acquired Tom's of Maine in 2006. That same year, L'Oreal acquired the Body Shop. Cadbury Schweppes purchased Green & Black's in 2005; Kraft Foods then took it over in 2010.

But more significantly, big brands are now turning to eco-business to re-design and reposition aspects and components of their mainstream brands to capture new sales. They are adopting the concept into their products to differentiate them and capture market share among a growing number of consumers who want healthier, safer, and more responsibly produced eco-friendly products without having to give up or pay more for their favorite brands. This is particularly the case in mature market segments where products compete mainly on price. Examples include household cleaners, detergents, packaged and processed foods, office supplies, and basic apparel. They are adopting regulated labels like "organic," as well as unregulated claims such as "green," "natural," "biodegradable," or "sustainably produced" (whether fully substantiated or not), to distinguish a branded product from the many otherwise similar competing items on the same retail shelf, and perhaps increase consumer interest and sales. In some cases the efforts are legitimate; in others, less so. In 2010, Ben & Jerry's voluntarily pulled the "all natural" claim from its ice cream label in response to a report that found that 48 of the company's 53 flavors had chemically modified ingredients.

Though eco-products remain far from perfect, companies such as Clorox are making some measurable improvements for business returns. This hundred-year-old brand leader in household cleaning products sells more than a billion items annually (such as Clorox bleach). When the company introduced its Greenworks line of "naturally derived," "plant-based" cleaning products in 2008, it probably had no idea that this would spur the adoption of eco-business goals throughout the entire business. Today Clorox claims it is committed to generating one-third of its growth from its eco-business efforts.

As many examples show, eco-business is accelerating because it is increasingly a means of innovation and competitive gains. Coca-Cola is emphasizing how a culture of environmental innovation will drive its future expansion, claiming it will focus on providing a new generation of younger consumers with more eco-friendly products. And General Electric's business plan positions its eco-business Ecomagination program as a driver for "reliable growth"; its annual revenue target from Ecomagination is now $25 billion, or 15.9 percent of the company's total revenue in fiscal year 2010.

The rise of eco-business is expanding markets and shifting them toward further big-brand advantage. With the repositioning of mainstream brands as eco-products, the lines between a sustainable product versus a product with some sustainable attributes are blurring, and the boundaries of eco-markets are growing. Green labels no longer necessarily signal a carefully crafted, low-impact, specialty item. Nor do they necessarily represent an inferior product that has sacrificed performance for a smaller environmental footprint (like phosphate-free detergents that leave spots on clothes, recycled-content bags that rip, or LED lights that are too dim).

For big-brand companies such as Nike, SC Johnson, and Samsung, product greening is at least partly concerned with innovating for quality and performance—seeking opportunities to redesign some brands to reduce costs and improve performance to gain market share. Nike's high-end 2010 FIFA World Cup soccer jerseys were light and durable, yet made from trash: the recycled material of 13 million plastic bottles recovered from landfills in Taiwan and Japan. SC Johnson's decision to remove volatile organic compounds from its top-selling

Windex cleaner decreased production costs, boosted Windex's cleaning power by 30 percent, and helped to increase market share. Samsung, meanwhile, is now selling a solar-powered laptop computer in the United States for about $400; first introduced in Africa, with great success, it has a screen that is 50 percent brighter than an average notebook to allow for easier use outdoors.

The paper company Cascades illustrates this trend further. It has invested in new technology to produce 100 percent recycled content toilet paper that is no longer "scratchy," but is instead as "plush" and "soft" as leading premium brands. For Cascades, the merging of sustainability with quality is part of an ambitious plan to vault its eco-friendly product line from its current lower-grade niche green market segment (2 percent of the overall tissue market) into the much larger higher value mainstream market in North America (with total annual tissue sales in North America of more than $6 billion).

Competing for Emerging Markets
Big-brand companies are not only leveraging eco-business to appeal to consumers in the mature markets of Western Europe and North America; they are also employing eco-business strategies to gain access to rapidly emerging markets, notably China, India, and Brazil. Although household incomes are lower in emerging economies, average annual GDP growth rates have been much higher in recent years: 8–12 percent compared with 1–4 percent in more developed economies. As was mentioned in chapter 2, by the year 2020, 60 percent of the billion or so new members of the global middle class will be in emerging economies. It is not surprising that big brands are eager to capture opportunities in those economies.

For big brands, country-level business risks and costs for poor infrastructure and logistics in developing countries are generally higher (e.g., poor highways, bridges, and airports to transport goods) than at home. Yet potential gains are also huge. Retail sales in China have been growing at rates as high as 20 percent. By 2009, Nokia, the world's largest cell phone manufacturer, was already selling three times as many phones in China as in the United States. In recent years IKEA has been opening 1–2 stores a year in China. Retailers like Walmart, Toys "Я" Us, and The Home Depot are increasing their presence mainly by partnering and acquiring domestic companies familiar with the local market, while brand manufacturers such as Coke, Unilever, and Adidas are relying on organic sales growth.[31]

Working alongside the global retail chains, big-brand manufacturers are setting aggressive sales targets in these new markets. Clorox plans to double its sales in Asia and Latin America within a decade. During this same period General Electric expects 60 percent of its revenue growth from sales in emerging markets. Unilever is aiming to sell its products to a billion new consumers in these fast-growing markets, with plans to expand its sales in China alone to $10 billion by 2020. Eco-business is crucial for achieving this projected growth. As Accenture found in a 2012 survey of 250 global-business executives, 64 percent reported that sustainability was essential to expanding their business into emerging economy markets, and 44 percent reported that they were already finding it hard to meet the demand for green products in these markets.[32]

Cutting waste to keep costs low is essential for entering markets where growth is fast but consumer incomes are low. Being innovative by regularly adapting with new products, processes, and business models is now also critical. Communicating "purpose" and "sustainability value," as was discussed in chapter 2, are increasingly central to how big brands are pursuing these strategies.

Choosing Environment *and* Profit?

"When sustainability burst onto the scene," explains Beth Lester, a vice-president at Lenn Schoen Berland Associates, "it was in the responsibility category, something that a company should do because it was the right thing to do. But now it is equally about saving money."[33]

Big-brand companies are using eco-business to achieve competitive goals: to lower costs and improve margins, to enhance product quality, to increase sales, and to grow markets. One aim is to expand and compete for eco-markets. Yet even bigger goals of eco-business are to improve quality, enhance marketability, and compete within mainstream markets. The result is both bottom-line efficiency and savings and top-line innovation and growth. Xerox executives explain this well in a covering letter for the company's 2009 Corporate Citizenship report: "Every one of our [sustainability] innovations ended up either saving us money or creating new markets and new revenue. We found, in other words, that we don't have to choose between the environment and profit. We can do both."[34]

Eco-business is helping big-brand companies to reduce the environmental impacts of some of their products. In at least some cases, the energy and material use per product sold is declining; so is the toxicity and percentage of waste going into landfills. But, as the many examples in this chapter show, "sustainability" is also helping the big brands to better compete to sell more. Eco-business frames the concept of sustainability around improved eco-efficiency, quality, and performance rather than around ecological constraints and limits. This is good for business, and big brands see this market advantage. Many also see even greater business gains than this chapter documents.

Big brands are now moving beyond their own operations and into their supply chains to multiply the competitive benefits from eco-business. Eco-business tools such as tracing, auditing, and labeling are providing big brands with greater power within supply chains. This is improving risk management and increasing overall productivity. And to some extent it is enhancing corporate accountability. Equally significant, it is also providing big-brand companies with greater control over product quality, price agreements, and supply-chain logistics— further boosting their business growth, governance credibility, and power over markets and sustainability.

4

Eco-Business Tools of Supply-Chain Power

In 2010, in an unprecedented move, Walmart gave notice to its more than 100,000 major suppliers that within the next five years it would be seeking to cut 20 million metric tons of carbon emissions from its supply chain. The consequence of not "helping out" was plain: risk being switched for a more compliant supplier. Soon after, IBM made a similar announcement, telling its 28,000 "first tier" suppliers in more than 90 countries that within a year they would have to implement a management system to track energy use, greenhouse-gas emissions, waste reduction, and recycling performance. They were also told to enforce the same policy for lower-tier subcontractors further up the supply chain. The consequence of not complying was again clear: risk being cut from the company's $40 billion global supply chain. Global companies now were competing hard to roll out supply-chain sustainability programs.

Why are these companies going beyond their own operations to impose sustainability requirements on their external suppliers? A central reason, we argue in this chapter, is control. Business tools of sustainability are proving to be a powerful way for big-brand companies to influence suppliers and mitigate supply-chain risks. With their viability anchored in global outsourcing, big brands need to engage effectively with

producers, manufacturers, and distributors at every stage along
their supply chains to remain competitive. Commenting on the
attributes of the world's top supply-chain performers, including Apple, Dell, and Procter & Gamble, Debra Hofman, research vice president at Gartner Inc., explains that "the key isn't
whether a company owns all the pieces of its network—it's how
it controls the outcome of the activities that take place in the
network that end in the delivery of a final product to a customer."[1] Big-brand companies are adopting various eco-business
tools and strategies to better orchestrate and increase this supply-chain power. Before explaining what these tools are and how
they work, we turn first to understanding supply chains, the role
of buyer power, and the increasing importance for big brands
of new management approaches to maintaining business value
in the face of growing global production and retail challenges.

Capturing Supply-Chain Value

Companies make, move, store, sell, reuse, recycle, and throw
away things through supply chains. Upstream producers and
manufacturers extract and transform natural resources and materials into finished products; distributors then deliver downstream to retailers who market the products to end consumers
for usage and disposal (and return) (figure 4.1). Management
of resources and relationships within these "value chains" of
activity, whether the business is a buyer or seller, can create big
losses or gains.[2] Effective management is therefore critical to
business success. And for big brands, the importance of doing
so is rising as these factors increasingly underpin their business
growth.

Supply-chain control can provide a decisive competitive advantage. Most business costs and environmental impacts for
most sectors are in the upstream supply chain (i.e., material

Upstream producers

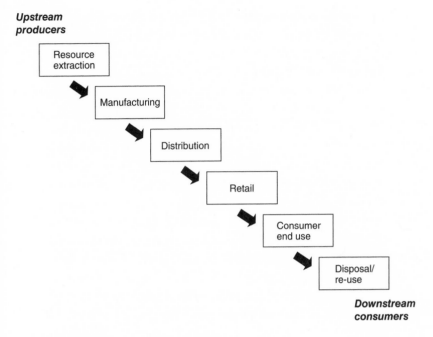

Downstream consumers

Figure 4.1
The upstream and downstream supply chain.

extraction and production stages). To enhance control, some companies vertically integrate, taking ownership of all of the stages of production, even downstream to the point of sale to the end customer. Mostly though, companies choose to specialize at one stage of the chain and then negotiate contractual procurement with other businesses to gain the greatest competitive positioning and returns. Some are highly decentralized. Disney, for example, rather than relying completely on its own manufacturing, grants licenses to thousands of different firms and factories worldwide to produce its trademarked toys, books, clothes, DVDs, and home furnishings. This is increasing profitability and flexibility. But it also makes Disney's supply chain

one of the longest and most intricate of any multinational corporation—and thus one of the most difficult to control.

The Influence of Big Brands

Many factors determine the degree of influence a company has
within a supply chain. The scale of the business, along with the
uniqueness of the company and its products, are of particular
importance. For instance, a producer with a large market share
of a rare material or specialized product will have more leverage—or "seller power"—than a supplier of a more homoge-
nized and easily substituted commodity or product (e.g., wood).

Over recent decades, as was detailed in chapter 2, big-brand
companies have accelerated growth and gained market dominance through supply-chain strategies that emphasize high-
volume, low-cost outsourcing. This has made big brands,
particularly multinational retailers, buyer powerhouses through
the sheer size of their purchases, revenues, and increasing market concentration. Walmart sits atop many of the world's
supply chains. More than 15 percent of the Chinese-made consumer goods (more than $30 billion) exported to the United
States each year head straight to a Walmart store.[3] Walmart's
Chinese suppliers, not surprisingly, were listening intently when
Walmart CEO Lee Scott told them in 2008 that they must now
comply with the company's sustainability requirements to remain Walmart suppliers. Walmart is simply too big a market
to ignore.

Output by a local producer can increase from 20,000 units
to 20 million units with a single big-brand contract. This can
leave a big-brand buyer accounting for a large share of sales
of a local business. A supplier, big or small, that relies on one
buyer for, say, 30 percent of its business can be left in a competitive market scramble to do whatever is necessary (legal or illegal) to maintain low prices and good relations with this buyer.

This is not to say that suppliers are powerless. But when a mass retail chain such as Walmart, Carrefour, or Best Buy places a huge product order, even the world's biggest companies can be left relying significantly on meeting this demand. Unilever, for example, has located its head office next to the headquarters of Asda (Walmart's British subsidiary) in Leeds, West Yorkshire. Procter & Gamble maintains an office in Walmart's hometown, Bentonville, Arkansas, with over 250 employees dedicated to managing its relationship with Walmart—15 percent of Procter & Gamble's market.

The economic power of big brands within global supply chains is growing as their sales and market reach expand.[4] Such power helps buyers to control costs and prices within supply chains. In an ideal, reinforcing cycle for the big-brand companies, supplier compliance further strengthens their control and market advantage. In reality, though, supplier compliance is far from perfect. Brand retail pressure is contributing to longer production chains as contracted manufacturers in turn seek to keep costs low by outsourcing to second-tier, third-tier, and fourth-tier subcontracted suppliers. As was noted earlier, this increases production risks and reduces the control of big-brand buyers. To mitigate and counteract this, big-brand companies are looking for new management tools and strategies like eco-business to help them maintain value from their supply chains. To better understand these tools, we first examine more closely the nature of some of the rising global supply-chain challenges and pressures arising from global outsourcing, activist campaigns, and regulations.

Managing Supply-Chain Risks

Supply chains are now like a "United Nations assembly of parts."[5] This has lowered the costs of goods sold, but it has also increased the risks of doing business. As supply chains lengthen, the "thin strands" become particularly difficult to manage. Potential deviation, disruption, and disaster are big concerns as global companies try to calculate the right balance between operating lean, cost-effective supply chains that limit suppliers, distances, and inventory and more robust supply-chain structures that can add redundancy and cost but provide greater contingencies given an unforeseen event.[6] Advocacy groups have responded to increasing product risks with campaigns that target products with unsustainable or harmful ingredients. And governments are implementing new regulations around supply-chain disclosure and accountability. Big brands are turning to eco-business supply-chain initiatives to help manage these rising challenges.

Risks Associated with Offshore Production

As the complexity and the length of supply chains increase, so does the risk of exposure and the challenge for a big brand of ensuring product quality, reliable delivery, and responsible practices. Many potentialities are beyond a firm's control, including natural disasters (earthquakes, tsunamis, floods, volcanic ash clouds), geopolitical disruptions (wars, piracy on the seas), and cyber-attacks (such as the one in 2011 on Sony's PlayStation Network, which compromised the personal information of 100 million customers and may end up costing the company up to $2 billion). A big-brand company can, however, potentially control and mitigate risks such as product defects and deviations.

Deviations in product quality and reliability that flow undetected through supply chains and surface during the retailing stage can saddle companies with millions in legal fees, lost inventory, disrupted production, and a decline in brand value. Problems such as defective batteries that catch fire and lead and cadmium in imported toys have cost Sony, Hewlett-Packard, Toshiba, Mattel, and Toys "Я" Us millions of dollars in fines, product recalls, shipment delays, and brand-defending public-relations campaigns.[7] More than 17 million toys and other consumer items, for example, were recalled in the United States in 2007 for violating federal standards regulating lead paint. Domestic suppliers are by no means fault-free. However, with so many consumer goods now flowing through China, and as global production shifts from China into even lower-cost locations (such as Lesotho and Bangladesh), risks such as these are amplified and come with hefty price tags. In just a single case in 2010, McDonald's had to pay millions to recall *Shrek Forever After* promotional cups that had been found to contain high levels of cadmium.

The market dynamics for honey demonstrate well why big-brand companies are pushing so hard for more supplier transparency and accountability. For the last ten years or so, customs officials and prosecutors in Europe and North America have been striving to shut down a global cartel of honey "launderers." Worldwide, beekeepers produce more than a million metric tons of honey per year. Much of the world's industrial honey—used in cereals, cookies, and cough drops—comes from China and is cheap by world standards. In the last two decades, import inspectors have repeatedly found that Chinese honey is diluted and impure, some of it contaminated with antibiotics banned in Europe and North America. The US government has also accused Chinese exporters of dumping honey to expand overseas markets. Facing a collapse of its domestic honey industry, in 2001 the United States put tariffs (antidumping duties) on honey imports from China. Today, as a result, it is rare for an American consumer to see honey with the label "Made in China." American honey imports come instead from Russia, India, Taiwan, Malaysia, the Philippines, and Indonesia—all places without much capacity to produce honey. American prosecutors now claim that much of this honey is actually from China, and that there is a worldwide laundering and food fraud operation to "clean" Chinese honey, with brokers from Germany and other countries repackaging and relabeling honey and falsifying papers.[8] Without doubt, the case for American prosecutors would benefit from a detailed mapping of the world's honey supply chains. Yet knowing this can also help brand manufacturers and retailers to maintain quality, manage risk, and avoid potential consumer scares for products that contain honey: a point that is true for hundreds of thousands of other products, too.

To protect brands and avoid such risks as illegal, low-quality inputs, companies are adopting a range of eco-business tools detailed in this chapter, including efforts to monitor, audit, and inspect products. Walmart announced in March 2011 that it would start doing its own testing of its products to check for toxics like polybrominated diphenyl ethers (PBDEs), carcinogenic flame retardants banned in the EU countries but still found in toys, sporting goods, pillows, mattresses, and furniture. Such voluntary efforts can increase a big-brand company's operating costs, but they also add strategic benefits by providing lead competitive positioning in the face of mounting advocacy and regulatory pressures to improve supply-chain responsibility.

Increasing Supply-Chain Activism

Big brands are increasingly accountable for and vulnerable to the practices of all the businesses that contribute to their products (regardless of the extent of ownership or investment). Focused and informed advocacy campaigns for greater accountability (on where and how products are made) are influencing consumers and governments and are putting pressure on big-brand companies to improve practices. Even smaller groups, using social media to raise awareness and mobilize large "flash mob" protests (such as those that occurred in 2011 at Apple retail stores across the United States), can rally worldwide interest and generate intense media coverage.

Activist groups have targeted Walmart for sourcing leather and beef from the deforested Amazon. Disney has been hit with allegations that the more than 50 million children's books and 30 million magazines it produces each year, and some of the packaging for its games and toys, are contributing to tropical deforestation. Activists have criticized Nestlé, Cadbury (acquired by Kraft in 2010), Mars, and Hershey for procuring unsustainable cocoa, and for buying palm oil for chocolate from Southeast Asian suppliers linked to degrading native forests and endangering wildlife habitats. Apple, Intel, and other electronics companies have been under pressure from advocacy groups to stop making cell phones, laptops, and cameras with "blood minerals" from conflict regions.

New Regulatory Requirements

In addition to the increasing activism, emerging supply-chain regulations are increasing risks for non-compliant brands. Governments are introducing laws and penalties to restrict chemicals, cut carbon, conserve water, reduce packaging, improve end-of-life management of products, and curtail trade in unsustainable products. The growing number of cases of "toxic toy" imports prompted the US government to introduce a new Product Safety law in 2008 banning lead and phthalates in products intended for children under the age of 12, and to strengthen the power of the US Consumer Product Safety Commission to test products and enforce standards. In addition, the amended Lacey Act in the US and a new due diligence directive in the EU both aim to prevent the import of illegal timber, and encourage companies to take more responsibility for the actions of their suppliers. The Dodd-Frank Wall Street Reform and Consumer Protection Act also imposes further supply-chain responsibility, requiring companies (particularly in the computer and electronics sectors) to conduct due diligence inquiries to trace the country-origin of gold, tin, tungsten, or tantalum to avoid conflict minerals in their products. Companies sourcing minerals originating from identified conflict regions are required to provide detailed reports. Across all levels of government, moreover, carbon regulations and policies are pending or being implemented that together pose a substantial risk for big-brand companies whose supply-chain management is inadequate.

Adaptive Response

To protect their brands from unnecessary costs and reputational damage from product defects and advocacy attacks, and to keep ahead of regulations, big brands are adapting eco-business policies and promises. In response to pressures, for example, Walmart claims it will now aim to stop purchasing beef and leather from illegally deforested land in the Amazon. After a public outcry, Cadbury reversed its decision to use palm oil instead of cocoa butter in its chocolate. After a YouTube video depicting a piece of a Kit Kat bar as an orangutan finger went viral, Nestlé dropped suspected suppliers and then committed to only using independently certified sustainably produced palm oil by 2015 (when it expects sufficient quantities to be available). And Apple and Intel (along with other electronics companies in the Electronic Industry Citizenship Coalition and global E-Sustainability Initiative) instituted a de facto procurement embargo to stop the trade in "conflict minerals" in the wake of protests accusing the industry of contributing to funding wars in Central Africa and degrading local environments.

More important, eco-business tools can help big-brand companies be proactive by anticipating and mitigating supply-chain risks rather than responding after reputational damage, fines, or market losses have already occurred.

Eco-Business Tools for Supply-Chain Control

The eco-business within supply chains varies somewhat across companies and industries. In more traditional business language, multinational corporations define sustainable supply-chain management in terms of "lean" cost-cutting efficiencies and "reverse logistics" business gains. Lean cost cutting involves identifying and eliminating unnecessary resources (measured in dollars, time, or raw materials). Reverse logistics involves recycling, reuse, and resale of products and materials to turn waste into profits back up through the supply chain. Big-brand companies are adopting a range of new eco-business tools that encompass both of these management strategies, designed to enhance their capacity to better govern and control supplier practices through all stages of production.[9] These include supply-chain tracing, life-cycle assessment, supplier codes and green procurement, auditing, certification, eco-labeling, and sustainability reporting.

Tracing

To manage supply chains well, companies first have to document them. In addition to understanding the primary suppliers with whom the company has direct purchase contracts, they also must understand the secondary and tertiary subcontracted suppliers upstream, the companies supplying the natural resources for all of the firms within the chain, and the downstream pathway of products to consumer usage and disposal. Tracing supply chains can be a difficult exercise. "We found

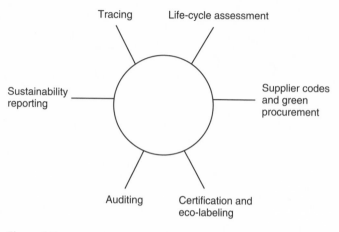

Figure 4.2
Eco-business tools for managing the supply chain.

that our supply chain goes farther than we imagined," Timberland's CEO Jeffrey Swartz discovered. "You have to go back to the cow."[10]

Among big brands, The Home Depot is a leader in supply-chain tracing. That wasn't always the case. In the late 1990s, the Rainforest Action Network and other environmental advocacy groups threatened to organize a boycott of Home Depot, Staples, and Office Depot stores unless those retailers started sourcing "sustainably produced" timber products. Executives, considering how to respond, began to ask themselves "What forests *do* our products come from?" They knew who their direct suppliers were. Yet their knowledge of the supply chain further upstream (where greater risks often lie) was limited.

Recognizing the growing importance of supply chains for brand reputations and markets, these companies, and an increasing number of others, set out to trace the thousands of products on their store shelves through each stage of production, right back to the sources of natural resources. Today, The

Home Depot boasts that it knows the forest source of every one of its timber products. Other big brands are now catching up. Adidas uses an online computer program it calls "String" to track the supply paths of the materials it uses. Walmart is promoting supply-chain transparency through its Selected Quality, Guaranteed Origin traceability program, launched by Walmart Brazil in August 2010, which enables suppliers and consumers to use a cell phone or the Walmart website to track the starting location and pathway of a product.

The complexity of a supply chain depends on many factors, including the size of the lead firm within a chain, the industry sector, and the product. A laptop computer has many more components than, say, a roll of toilet paper or a T-shirt. Yet tracing the precise source of the raw materials can be surprisingly difficult even for relatively simple products. Levi Strauss discovered this when tracing the components of its 501 jeans. The cotton was grown in the Mississippi Delta region. The fabric was woven in North Carolina. The jeans were sewn in Haiti and finished in the Dominican Republic. Even this was only a fraction of the chain. The grommets, buttons, thread, zippers, and rear pocket patches came from different countries worldwide.

Mapping supply chains can help to reduce the complexity of supply structures as well as enable greater control by identifying the various players, processes, and potential partners. Big-brands are putting efforts into tracing to increase their awareness and understanding of how their products are flowing from the environment to the store shelf. But this knowledge alone doesn't ensure reliable or responsibly produced supplies. Although it can help a company to avoid procuring illegal materials and products from controversial regions or suppliers, simply knowing where a product comes from doesn't reveal the impacts of producing it. To do this, the companies are turning to other eco-business tools, such as life-cycle assessment, eco-certification, and auditing.

Life-Cycle Assessment

Supply-chain tracing identifies companies and processes. Life-cycle analysis (LCA) evaluates their consequences. Big-brand companies are employing LCA to weigh and measure things like carbon, energy, water, and material usage within products and processes through all stages of the supply chain, from extraction through manufacturing, distribution, retail, consumer usage, and disposal. (See figure 4.3.) Levi Strauss discovered that making one pair of 501 jeans required 1.7 pound of cotton and more than 1,700 liters of water. The life-cycle of a pair of jeans produced more than 32 kilograms of carbon dioxide, roughly equal to driving a car 78 miles. The majority of this greenhouse impact was found to occur during the consumer usage stage—mainly from using electric clothes dryers.[11]

Life-cycle analysis calculations can be complex. Many software packages and databases are available to help, however, such as Earthster's open-source ones piloted by Walmart, Seventh Generation, and TetraPak. In addition, there are technical documents (e.g., ISO 14040) and LCA tools (such as those developed by the Sustainability Consortium and Global Packaging Project). As yet, however, no standard LCA methodology exists. Life-cycle analysis is nevertheless helping the big brands to identify where and how they can make the greatest environmental advances along the supply chain and how they can gain more knowledge so as to enhance their influence over suppliers. In 2007, Drew Schram, a senior vice president with the furniture firm Herman Miller, gave a sense of the mood of buyers in a comment to a *New York Times* reporter: "Carbon footprint is absolutely new territory. We're not sure how we'll

Stages

Impacts

- Land use intensity
- Biodiversity
- Waste
- Water
- Energy
- Chemistry/toxics
- Greenhouse gas emissions

Figure 4.3
Life-cycle assessment: stages and impacts.

measure it, we're not sure how we'll deal with it, but we've told our suppliers, 'Get ready, because we're going to ask you a lot of questions.'"[12]

Life-cycle analysis can help big-brand companies to find more efficient ways to move toward eco-business targets. Walmart is pushing its suppliers to cut 20 million tons of carbon emissions by 2015 after reportedly calculating that these suppliers account for 90 percent of the company's total carbon footprint. Similarly, Timberland's focus on resource efficiency is driven by its LCA claim that most of its carbon footprint comes from activities before they even start to make apparel items such as shoes.

Many other big brands are taking a similar approach. Apple has implemented a supplier code of conduct and is conducting compliance audits after calculating and claiming that its own facilities account for just 3 percent of its carbon footprint. Virtually all big brands are now using LCA data to point a finger at suppliers and roll out new purchasing rules on aspects such as carbon, toxics, and conflict materials—important for managing supply-chain impacts but also for protecting brand reputation and ensuring product quality.

Not only is life-cycle analysis helping big brands to reveal upstream opportunities with suppliers; it is also helping downstream to better position products with customers. Levi Strauss, for example, used their 501 jeans LCA analysis to team up with other big retailers (including Gap, IKEA, and H&M) on the Better Cotton Initiative, an effort to produce and trade cotton "more sustainably." In addition, Levi Strauss began promoting cold-water detergent in partnership with Procter & Gamble after reported results that significant downstream impacts came from consumers washing its jeans in energy-wasting hot water. Most fundamentally, though, Levi Strauss is using LCA data to improve its upstream supply-chain performance to keep its downstream prices low so as to maintain its high-volume contract with Walmart—the exclusive retailer of its lower-end Levi's Signature jeans.

Recognizing the eco-business value of life-cycle analysis, companies are establishing databases of detailed information on products and suppliers. As part of its Sustainability Index, Walmart is working with a "sustainability consortium" that includes other big-brand companies, universities, governments, and non-governmental organizations to create a global database of the life-cycle environmental impacts of consumer products. The stated aim (still a long way off) is to put more detailed information on labels so as to reduce a product's downstream footprint by helping consumers make better choices.

In another initiative, a hundred outdoor apparel and retail companies, including Patagonia, North Face, and Timberland, have created a software tool called the Eco Index. Similar to Walmart's Sustainability Index, it aims to measure the environmental impact of footwear and apparel through the product life cycle. The brands ask their suppliers a range of questions about their environmental practices; the answers are then translated into a gold, silver, or bronze ranking. The Eco Index provides big-brand companies with strategic information that can enhance their capacity to influence supplier practices. Suppliers participate to retain business.

Timberland's senior manager of environmental stewardship, Betsy Blaisdell, claims that the Eco Index has prompted the company to look for leather tanneries with less environmentally damaging business practices. This in turn, is spurring competition among suppliers to declare "corporate responsibility"—and perhaps even improve practices. "I now have tanneries," says Blaisdell, "fighting over the points needed to get a silver rating."[13]

In 2011, clothing retailers, manufacturers, environmental groups, and academics formed the Sustainable Apparel Coalition. Its founding members include Walmart, Target, J. C. Penny, Adidas, Nike, and Timberland. This group also includes environmental NGOs, labor rights groups, and government bodies. The stated aim is to encourage sustainable manufacturing and better inform consumers of the ecological impact of clothing. The coalition is developing a sustainability indexing tool (the "Higg Index") that companies will be able to use to score all the players within the clothing supply chains, including cotton growers, fabric makers, dye suppliers, and textile owners, as well as packagers, shippers, retailers, and consumers. In theory, the indexing tool can evaluate labor and land-use practices, greenhouse-gas emissions, waste practices, and chemical, energy, and water usage, one day providing (if the partners can agree on it) a tool for giving a garment a sustainability score that can then be put on its label. This will benefit consumers, but, more importantly for the big brands, it will provide a wealth of strategic information about their suppliers.

Supplier Codes and Green Procurement

Tracing and life-cycle analysis help big-brand companies to set supply-chain targets. Supplier codes of practice as well as procurement programs and contracts provide a vehicle for them to operationalize new requirements for suppliers. Hewlett-Packard, the world's largest computer company, was the first in its sector to develop a sustainability code for its suppliers; it was also a leading advocate behind the establishment of the Electronic Industry Code of Conduct. Suppliers comply out of both opportunity (the opportunity of getting a large sales contract for meeting the criteria) and fear (the fear of losing out or being switched for a more compliant competitor). Such codes and policies are partly about lessening the environmental footprint of the company's products and reducing risk, but even more about lowering costs, improving product quality, and increasing productivity by changing supplier practices. (See chapter 5.) Retailers' policies for buying timber are illustrative.

Spurred by pressure from NGOs, The Home Depot and Staples were among the first big-brand retailers to implement wood and paper procurement policies to prohibit timber purchases from endangered forest regions and to give preference to timber products certified as "sustainable." The Home Depot did so in 1999, Staples in 2002. Since then, all of the big-brand do-it-yourself home improvement, office supply, and mega-hypermarket (e.g., Walmart) retailers have followed suit. Tools like the World Business Council for Sustainable Development's *Sustainable Procurement of Wood and Paper-based Products Guide* are helping buyers to source more strategically. Hundreds of the world's leading brands are also participating in the Consumer Goods Forum, which passed a resolution in November 2010 committing its members to achieving zero deforestation within a decade by avoiding the purchase of paper, beef, soy, and palm oil products from native tropical forests. And the Forest Footprint Disclosure Project, launched in the UK in 2009 with the backing of 36 institutional investors with assets of more than $4 trillion, is helping big brands to move toward zero deforestation by tracing the global supply chains of "forest risk commodities."

Some big-brand companies have also adopted policies to avoid purchasing some threatened fish species. In the United States, Walmart and Sam's Club committed themselves in 2006 to selling only wild-caught and frozen fish (as certified by the Marine Stewardship Council) by the end of 2011. As of October 2011 McDonald's has publicly committed to selling only MSC-certified fish fillets at its 7,000 restaurants across 39 European countries. That represents about 100 million "Filet-o-Fish" servings a year.

Although definitions vary and underlying criteria for what qualifies as "sustainable" are often unclear, many of the big supermarkets are also now claiming to give more preference to "organic," "locally produced," and "sustainably produced" seafood, meat, eggs, dairy, fruit, bread, and vegetables. Walmart, the world's biggest grocer, announced in 2010 that by 2015 it would double its annual sales of locally produced foods in the United States, and would source food from a million small and medium-size farms worldwide. Carrefour, already France's top seller of organic food, is promising to do more to promote sustainable and local purchasing. It reports that it sells more than 20 different MSC-certified products and more than 3,700 organic products in its stores worldwide, many of them under its private label, AGIR Eco Planète. Other firms have also recently made ambitious promises. Unilever, for example, claims that it is now aiming to achieve 100 percent "sustainable agriculture sourcing" by 2020.

Big-brand companies are developing, implementing, and sharing supplier scorecards to help them better access and evaluate sourcing options. In addition, they are participating in "buyer-group" initiatives to watch for illegal activities and help with more "responsible" procurement. The Global Forest and Trade Network, for example, is aiming to expand the world market for "environmentally responsible forest products" by linking up companies, NGOs, and communities across more than 30 countries. The more recently formed European Timber Retail Coalition also brings together big-brand European retailers—including Carrefour, Kingfisher, IKEA, and Marks & Spencer—to help these companies avoid importing illegal timber into the EU market. Similar initiatives in other industries (e.g., the Better Cotton Initiative in the apparel sector) are beginning to change business practices within supply chains.

Fundamentally, supplier codes and green procurement provide an additional lever for big-brand companies to reshape supplier practices in their own image—namely, low-cost, efficient, and reliable production. Introducing codes and guidelines into supply chains adds a new business challenge, however: confirming whether suppliers are obeying.

Auditing
Credibility and trust are integral to brand reputation and loyalty. The sale of faulty or contaminated products sourced from any supplier (whether directly or subcontracted further up the chain) can send a big-brand company's stock price tumbling. A track record for environmental measures within a corporation's own operations doesn't protect it from such fallout. Meeting only some of its corporate environmental commitments also leaves a company vulnerable.

Dell, the world's third-largest computer manufacturer, was reminded of this when dealing with the Greenpeace "What the Dell" campaign, the point of which was to push the company to do more to "green" its electronics. In May 2010, Greenpeace

USA activists scaled Dell's headquarters in Round Rock, Texas, to hang a banner addressed to founder Michael Dell; the banner read "MICHAEL, WHAT THE DELL? DESIGN OUT TOXICS!" Even though Dell's overall sustainability efforts were generally ahead of those of its main competitors, Greenpeace was taking Dell to task for failing to meet its 2009 commitment to phase out PVC vinyl plastic and brominated flame retardants from all of its computer products. This was a perfectly reasonable demand, Greenpeace activists emphasized, insofar as Apple and Hewlett-Packard were already marketing products without those chemicals. Dell ended up scrambling to reassure consumers of its continued commitment to deliver on its promise. Although Dell, like its competitors, is still far from fully phasing out the use of toxic materials in its computers (antimony and beryllium compounds and phthalates still remain), Dell has demonstrated progress, moving within a year from tenth to second place in Greenpeace's November 2011 *Guide to Greener Electronics* ranking.

In 2011, it was alleged that Mattel was contributing to tropical deforestation by sourcing native tropical hardwood fiber for the packaging for its toys. Greenpeace had done forensic testing on the paper packaging and had determined that at least some of the fibers had come from native Indonesian forests. Activists converged on Mattel's headquarters in Los Angeles dressed as Ken dolls in baby blue tuxedos and hung a huge banner declaring "BARBIE, IT'S OVER. I DON'T DATE GIRLS THAT ARE INTO DEFORESTATION." Hundreds of thousands of supporters subsequently joined the campaign's Facebook page. In response, Mattel announced that it was enhancing its LCA program by adding a purchasing policy to address deforestation in the supply chains of all its product lines, including requirements for its packaging suppliers to commit to sustainable forest-management practices. It also publicly launched its own investigation into the deforestation allegations against its packaging supplier.

Big brands continue to monitor closely—and sometimes react to—such advocacy campaigns, but now they have another worry. An individual, whether an industry pundit or a concerned teenager, now can post damaging evidence (true or not) on YouTube, Facebook, or Twitter, and reach millions of people, harming a brand overnight. Companies recognize that more than ever they need to be proactive.

To help protect their brands and stay ahead of controversies and complaints, big-brand companies are going to increasing lengths, as was explained earlier, to oversee and track their supply chains right back to the local producer and subcontracted suppliers. They are also going to considerable efforts to report on their supply-chain performance and progress toward goals and targets. They are implementing audit programs, hiring third-party auditors, and partnering with environmental groups such as Conservation International and The Nature Conservancy to check up on supplier practices and compliance. Though auditing efforts may well not produce better outcomes for the ecosystems surrounding local suppliers, big-brand companies nevertheless see it as a valuable eco-business tool for overseeing suppliers' practices and their compliance with quality standards.[14]

IKEA's code of conduct for its suppliers—called IWAY—commits the company to auditing its wood supply chain and its paper, food, and textile suppliers. In 2010, out of a total of 117 audits, IKEA's internal team audited more than 80 wood suppliers in China, including a few unannounced audits by external third-party auditors. Walmart and The Home Depot are undertaking similar efforts. As a consequence, in the course of a single year some of the big manufacturers in China now have dozens of audit teams from different big-brand companies coming through their factories. Most suppliers in China still get missed, however: the sheer number of small firms; the highly fragmented structure of production; and skilled supplier efforts to obfuscate their operations mean, at best, big brands' auditing is only skimming the surface of suppliers' practices. As of 2011, only 16 percent of IKEA's wood supply came from audit-verified "preferred" sources.[15]

To enhance supply-chain management capacity and control, big brands are also developing other tools to impose rules, encourage standardized techniques and cooperation, and verify supplier practices. The most common tool is certification.

Certification and Eco-Labeling

The use of certification programs to promote "sustainable production" is increasing in all sectors of the world economy. (See table 4.1.) This includes the well-developed certification programs for forest and paper products, organically grown agricultural products, and seafood and the newly emerging ones for conflict-free minerals and sustainable soy, palm oil, and biofuels. Through independent third-party audits based on a checklist of criteria, certification provides buyers with a way to increase their control over the procurement and production of products.[16] In an increasing number of cases, big-brand companies are working to assist their suppliers with certification. For example, IKEA, recognizing its exposure to illegally sourced wood fiber, is working with the WWF to help increase the number of certified Chinese wood and paper suppliers.

Big brands are adopting certification to better control suppliers' practices and to boost profitability. Chiquita's partnership with the Rainforest Alliance in the 1990s to certify their banana crops, for example, introduced new practices to better protect local ecosystems that reportedly also increased farm productivity by 27 percent and reduced costs by 12 percent.[17]

Table 4.1
Certification standards and eco-labels for consumer goods.

Sector	Common certifications and eco-labels
Apparel	Organic (cotton)Bluesign
Electronics	ENERGY STAR EPEAT
Food & Beverage	Fairtrade Organic Marine Stewardship Council Rainforest Alliance UTZ Certified
Household & Personal Care	AISE Eco-Cert Fairtrade Organic Nordic Swan EcoLogo Green Seal
Office Supply (paper & furniture)	Forest Stewardship Council (FSC) Programme for the Endorsement of Forest Certification (PEFC) Sustainable Forestry Initiative (SFI) Canadian Standards Association Z809 (CSA)

Adapted from *Signed, Sealed, Delivered? Behind Certifications and Beyond Labels* (SustainAbility, 2011), p. 11.

Big-brand companies are also using certification as a way to establish "green credibility" and capture the growing demand for environmentally friendly products. The range of certification programs is increasing quickly, and many of these programs include eco-labeling options. To scale up these programs, companies are participating in initiatives (such as the Global Eco-labelling Network) that help to standardize life-cycle analysis methods and metrics and to verify and communicate the eco-friendly aspects of consumer brands.

Governments have well-established green label programs. The European Union's standardized Eco-Flower logo and the US ENERGY STAR program are two global leaders. Since 2000 consumers have bought more than 3 billion products with an ENERGY STAR label. The amount of greenhouse-gas emissions avoided in 2010 alone, ENERGY STAR claims, is equal to taking 33 million cars off the road.

Third-party auditing, certification, and eco-labeling programs are not without their challenges and critics (e.g., with respect to consistency and fairness), and challenges and criticisms can present risks to big-brand companies. In response, big brands are launching a growing array of their own logos and labels (some legitimate and some not) to advertise and promote so-called sustainable products. In some cases, this is enabling brands to define and gain market control over the sustainability standards by which consumers will judge their products—for example, the definitions and expectations for recyclability, recycled content, organic, carbon neutral, and energy and water efficiency. Some retailers, including Tesco, are planning to go even further, aiming for product labels that will enable consumers to compare things like "carbon footprint" as easily as they can compare price or nutritional profile.[18]

The market, as a consequence, is becoming increasingly crowded with a confusing array of legitimate and illegitimate green claims and labels, which is leaving even loyal eco-brand buyers baffled. Although additional product information improves transparency, it can be difficult to interpret. Specifically, rating the most environmentally friendly product by calculating and weighing the tradeoffs among different attributes can be difficult, as the examples in table 4.2 show.

To overcome the risk of confusing consumers and potentially losing trust and sales, some brands are trying to assist by developing sustainability indices and simple rating systems

Table 4.2
Weighing consumption tradeoffs.

Product	Environmental improvement	Questionable overall gain
Plastic Water Bottle	100% recyclable	How green when 80% of water bottles are not recycled?
Compact Fluorescent Bulb	Uses 75% less energy	Is it worth the risk of mercury exposure from a broken bulb?
Barbie Doll	Accessories made from recycled fabric from other dolls	How green if the origin of the doll's apparel is unknown?
Toothpaste	Lightweight tube saves energy in shipping	Are energy savings offset by the cardboard packaging it comes in?
Dish Soap	80% shipped on biodiesel trucks	Did the biodiesel come from producers that cleared forests for palm and other oils?
T-shirt	5% organic cotton	How green given that growing cotton uses a lot of water?

Adapted from Paul Keegan, "The Trouble with Green Product Ratings," *Fortune*, July 25, 2011, pp. 130–134.

(as described earlier). They are also making efforts to publicize their corporate sustainability efforts, including efforts to increase the accountability and transparency of suppliers.

Reporting

Demands for more corporate transparency are rising, particularly in the area of sustainability. Increasingly, consumers, communities, NGOs, governments, employees, and investors expect companies to be more open, not just about financial matters, but also about environmental goals, challenges, and progress.

Addressing corporate executives, Patricia Jurewicz, director of the Responsible Sourcing Network, summed this up well in 2011: "Whether you like it or not, this transparency tsunami is coming and you better be prepared for it." Pressed on how far supply-chain transparency would need to go, she replied "Down to the dirt."[19]

To maintain credibility and brand trust, and to counter charges of greenwashing, many companies are publishing sustainability information. This includes sharing information about their greenhouse-gas emissions and their carbon footprint. Tesco now posts its emissions data online to enable anyone to track the company's assessment of its progress toward its goal of reducing its carbon emissions by 50 percent by 2020. Many companies are also adopting standards such as the Global Reporting Initiative when they compile their annual sustainability reports. According to the consulting firm KPMG, 85 percent of the world's 250 biggest companies now use the GRI reporting framework.[20]

To enhance the credibility of such voluntary reporting, many big brands are hiring independent auditing firms, such as PricewaterhouseCoopers and Deloitte, to verify the accuracy of reported information (as defined by the company). Increasingly, sustainability reporting and corporate communications with consumers are also moving online. Companies are participating in social media and launching interactive websites. Many sites now provide case-study videos, interactive question-and-answer games about the company and its products, and "dashboards" featuring detailed metrics and charts on a company's sustainability performance. Marks & Spencer even offers "My Plan A," which allows consumers to pledge to live a "sustainable lifestyle." A 2010 survey of 75 global companies found that 81 percent now have sustainability information on their websites, 33 percent include videos, 28 percent have blogs, and

24 percent are using social networks to communicate sustainability efforts in a favorable light.[21] The trend toward greater corporate transparency of sustainability metrics is accelerating. For example, in 2003 fewer than 20 percent of the global 500 companies reported their carbon emissions to the Carbon Disclosure Project. Seven years later, about 75 percent of them were reporting.[22]

This trend is extending, too, as big-brand companies look to reassure customers by expanding transparency efforts into supply chains. Dole now links its website to Google Earth so that viewers can see a farm in Peru where it is buying "organic" bananas. Disney customers can track their Mickey Mouse T-shirt online through all its stages of production by logging their T-shirt tag number into www.trackmyt.com. Apple has recently joined Hewlett-Packard and Dell in revealing the names of global suppliers.

Big brands are using eco-business tools to gain greater supply-chain transparency to help them meet stakeholders' expectations and convince customers that the company's sustainability commitments are meaningful. They are rolling out sustainability reporting through supply chains to help build and maintain brand trust by providing a picture of the company's progress toward its goals. The companies are also using this supplier knowledge strategically to help them to better select suppliers as well as direct—and improve—the processes and products within their supply chains.

The Rising Power of Eco-Business

In a growing number of instances, the eco-business of supply-chain management is helping to raise corporate standards. And at least in some cases big-brand companies are extending life-cycle assessments, codes, audits, certification, eco-labels, tracing, and reporting into their supply chains in ways that are encouraging better corporate environmental practices. Yet it is important to keep in mind that big brands are doing this primarily to increase their control over the supply chain.

In the face of mounting risks of product defects and production disruptions, advocacy attacks over irresponsible sourcing, and new government regulations calling for greater accountability, eco-business tools are providing big brands with more capability to track their many suppliers, and obtain information about their practices—both legal and illegal. Such knowledge increases the ability of big-brand companies to respond to increasing demands for transparency and accountability. It also allows them to better control their suppliers by rewarding and strengthening ties with high performers while screening out and holding lagging suppliers more accountable for poor practices or quality inconsistencies. At the same time, big brands are directly channeling this capacity into business growth, using eco-business to push down supplier costs even further and to offer even lower prices to increasing numbers of discount shoppers.

5

The Supply-Chain Eco-Business of Brand Growth

Business efforts within a company's own operations are important, but ultimately greater business gains can come from reaching further. Financially successful companies know this and see their supply chains as crucial value chains with the strategic potential to multiply financial returns through better management and cooperation. Yet before about 2005 most multinational corporations were not monitoring or attempting to govern the sustainability performance of their supply chains. This was true for the impacts of upstream resource extraction and material processing as well as for downstream consumer use (something traditionally seen as beyond the control of big brands). Much has changed since then. As was made clear in the preceding chapter, big-brand companies are now adopting ambitious supply-chain sustainability goals and employing a range of new eco-business tools to develop energy, carbon, water, and waste requirements through all stages of the product life cycle as a means for monitoring distant producers and suppliers to manage product risks and enhance control.

In this chapter, we probe more deeply into the business value gains big-brand companies are pursuing by channeling eco-business up and down the supply chain. In particular, we investigate how big brands are leveraging eco-business here to increase brand value and promote growth. This includes harnessing it to help stabilize resource supplies, improve product quality and productivity, lower costs, and connect better with consumers. As John Coyne of Unilever Canada explains, supply-chain sustainability efforts are helping to "protect and enhance Unilever's reputation, secure supply for our business over the long term, help provide increased stability of operations, and create cost efficiencies." "Ultimately," Coyne continues, "they generate competitive advantage."[1]

Securing Resources

Within supply chains, speed, agility, efficiency, responsiveness, and innovation provide big brands with competitive advantages. Resilience, too, is an important competitive advantage. This is not just about having the flexibility to rebound from an unpredictable natural disaster that disrupts global supply lines and material flows. It is equally about being able to respond to global economic challenges, such as tightening resource supplies, high commodity price volatility, and looming scarcities for important inputs such as oil and water.

In 2010, for example, oil prices rose by more than 17 percent, sugar prices by more than 25 percent, and wheat prices by nearly 50 percent. And cotton hit a fifteen-year high.[2] Securing stable supplies of even basic raw materials (e.g., water, metals, timber, and food) is an increasing business priority. John Brock, CEO of Coca-Cola, expressed the worry and potential competitive advantages of embracing corporate sustainability back in 2008:

[W]e've had some real issues with the price of high fructose corn syrup, similarly, with the price of aluminum which goes into cans, which make up 60% of our products in North America, as well as petroleum, which, of course has been volatile. . . . That affects our fuel prices, but it also goes into our plastic bottles. . . . So we've had major challenges from a commodity price standpoint for the last three years. Very different than the previous twenty five years. . . . Sustainability is critical, absolutely key.[3]

In order to understand and quantify the uncertainties and challenges regarding their impacts and dependencies on resources and natural environments, big-brand companies are beginning to use corporate ecosystem reviews and valuation frameworks, such as those developed by the World Business Council on Sustainable Development and the World Resources Institute. These frameworks are helping them, for example in the case of timber, to assess the impacts of products and packaging on forests, and the ability of forest ecosystems to stabilize water tables and local climates, purify water, and provide flood protection, soil stability, and carbon sequestration. In 2011, Puma drew positive attention (particularly from investors) with the production of its first corporate "environmental profit and loss" statement. The purpose, Puma explained, was to help the company to identify the cost of its impact and reliance on natural resources and integrate it into its business planning in order to help it maintain reliable returns and long-term value. Other big brands are now participating in similar pilot projects, some through the World Business Council for Sustainable Development's Corporate Ecosystem Valuation Project.

The Gartner consulting firm found in its 2011 ranking of the leading global supply-chain companies that a crucial lesson from today's top financial performers is that the need to "deliver predictable results, despite the volatility . . . is now here to stay."[4] Puma and many other big brands are implementing eco-business within their supply chains to attempt to smooth the up and down cycles and better anticipate and reduce the associated costs from environmental change and resource scarcities. They are aiming to use eco-business strategies to increase their business intelligence about suppliers and their resilience to better manage and cope with looming constraints around even their most basic commodity supplies.

Managing Supply Constraints

As consumption rises worldwide with expanding populations and development, regional demand-supply imbalances are growing and resource supplies are tightening. Companies across all sectors are concerned about the reliability and security of future supplies and about access to materials. Rare earth metals in the technology sector are illustrative. Wind turbines, electric motors, and missiles all require them. So do many consumer goods, including smart phones, hard disks, and compact fluorescent bulbs. Yet, while the demand for such metals is widespread, a single country, China, controls about 95 percent of the world's supply. This leaves firms vulnerable to the politics of the day. As was mentioned in chapter 1, in 2010 the Chinese government imposed a 2-month embargo on rare earth metal and mineral exports to Japan; the government also prevented some shipments to Europe and North America. This further constrained global supplies and drove world prices to record levels. In response, companies are now working with suppliers to reduce reliance and increase recovery from discarded devices. In one small example, Hitachi has developed a process to recover rare earth magnets from the disks and compressors of old computers and is intending to start full operational rare material recycling in 2013. Big-brand companies are also researching and developing alternative supplies. One innovative idea is "bioleaching," in which rock-eating bacteria that thrive in acidic environments extract rare minerals from low-grade ore.[5]

Even more commonplace, household staples such as honey, cocoa, and coffee are experiencing global shortages, illegal trading, and quality problems. This is spurring big brands to implement supply-chain eco-business strategies to offset increasing prices and to try to lock in volume and quality guarantees. For example, in recent years Côte D'Ivoire and Ghana together have been producing more than half of the world's traded cocoa beans. Political unrest and environmental decline in those countries are contributing to high global market volatility for cocoa. Civil unrest and continuing declines in productivity have caused cocoa prices to rise and supplies to become even more unstable. Prices hit a 30-year high in 2010. Meanwhile, consumer demand for chocolate is outpacing cocoa production.

The world's biggest chocolate buyers, including Kraft, Hershey, Mars, and Nestlé, have been scrambling to develop strategies to deal with these problems and are leveraging supply-chain sustainability to help. Mars, for example, promised in 2009 to buy all of its chocolate products from "sustainable sources" by 2020. Such goals are facing large ongoing hurdles, though; for instance, since 2009 the European Union has put in place sanctions for doing business with Côte D'Ivoire, and the United States has supported a ban on cocoa exports from the country. Shifting to what Mars calls sustainable sources would cost the company tens of millions of dollars over the next decade. Nonetheless, according to Howard-Yana Shapiro, the global director of plant science for Mars, "it is the appropriate choice for a stable, high-quality cocoa supply in the future."[6] Mars is now working with its cocoa suppliers and with the Rainforest Alliance to improve the practices of cocoa farmers. The company has also invested $10 million in a 5-year project to improve productivity by mapping the entire cocoa genome to develop trees that can better survive drought and disease. Chris Wille, chief of sustainable agriculture for the Rainforest Alliance, explains: "The chocolate industry, like the coffee sector, is quickly waking up to the fact that they need to address their supply chain all the way back to the farmers because if not, they may not have all the raw ingredients . . . they need."[7]

Big brands, the case of cocoa reveals, are working with and monitoring suppliers to help protect the corporate bottom line by enhancing their capacity to avoid shortages. Unilever assisted in creating the Marine Stewardship Council in part to encourage "sustainable" management of depleting fish stocks but also for competitive reasons: to maintain a stable supply to its factories packaging frozen fish. Faber-Castell has had its Brazilian pine plantation eco-certified by the Forest Stewardship Council in part to promote a reliable, low-cost, high-quality, and local supply of fiber for its pencil plant in São Carlos, Brazil (the world's largest, producing more than 2 billion pencils a year). In other sectors, too, big brands are increasing their efforts to lock in supplies of "sustainably produced" inputs. PepsiCo has a partnership with the Inter-American Development Bank to invest $2.6 million to establish a trustworthy and consistent supply of sunflower oil from Mexico for its potato chips, cookies, nuts, and other snacks. Unilever is looking to reduce its palm oil use by investing in substitutes, such as the seeds of the Allanblackia tree in Africa. Both companies participate, along with Marks & Spencer, Costco, Mars, and Starbucks, in the multistakeholder Sustainable Food Laboratory, an organization set up to foster supply-chain innovations for climate, soil, poverty, and water issues to encourage healthier and more secure and reliable food production, distribution, and sale.

Although supply pressures are growing in many areas, perhaps the most pervasive, consequential, and immediate resource shortage concerns fresh water. Most companies, a 2011 corporate survey found, have yet to respond with adequate measures.[8] Of those claiming to take a leadership role, however, many are big brands. These companies, almost without exception, now see long-term business value from better managing this resource.

Conserving the Last Drops

The manufacturing of every consumer good requires water. As supplies of clean fresh water in many regions dwindle with changes in climate and with rising agricultural and industrial demands, companies are adopting supply-chain strategies to reduce the amount of pollution and water consumption, not just in their own facilities (see chapter 3), but during all stages of production. CEOs of major brands have signed on to the UN Global Compact's CEO Water Mandate to improve global water stewardship. Industry-wide tools such as the Global Environmental Management Initiative's Water Sustainability Tool are helping to define water opportunities and risks through the supply chain. Companies are also establishing their own initiatives. In 2009, in partnership with the WWF, the brewing conglomerate SABMiller carried out the first comprehensive water footprint analyses, calculating the life-cycle water impacts of its beer operations in South Africa and the Czech Republic from crop cultivation to brewing to distribution. In India, among its water-conservation efforts, Hindustan Unilever (India's largest consumer-goods company) has launched an initiative called India Water Body—a nationwide survey to assess, monitor, and help mitigate the anticipated gap in India's water future.[9] The public goal of the project is to help the country manage its water resources; it will also, however, provide the company with information crucial to long-term competitive positioning.

Water quality and shortages aren't a problem only in water-scarce developing regions (such as Central Africa and Southern India) or in arid developed countries such as Australia. France, Brazil, and other countries experiencing droughts have been rationing supplies. In the US, the General Accounting

Office was estimating in 2003 that 36 of the states would face water shortages by 2013; that prediction came true five years sooner.[10] Warning signs appeared even earlier. In 2001, Nestlé was drawn into a multi-million-dollar court battle with a community group in Michigan over the level and impacts of its withdrawals of fresh water for its local bottled-water plant. And in the same year, the brewer Anheuser-Busch suffered large business losses when a drought in the Pacific Northwest disrupted the supply chains for barley and aluminum. More recently, Nestlé abandoned plans to build a huge water-bottling plant in California owing to that state's growing water scarcity.

Across all sectors and jurisdictions there are a growing number of examples of big-brand companies working to better monitor supply chains for water quantity and quality, putting in place reporting systems to improve early warning and control over potential upstream shortages that might affect production. Campbell's, for example, is working with the University of California at Davis and local farmers to conduct field experiments and monitor water use. Similarly, PepsiCo has worked with Cambridge University to develop a web-based soil moisture sensing technology called "i-crop." PepsiCo's suppliers now use the tool to monitor and manage water consumption, allowing the head office to keep close tabs on progress and any emerging supply disruptions.

PepsiCo's biggest competitor, Coca-Cola, is implementing water-related eco-business through its supply chains with equal vigor. Protests and threats of forced plant closures have spurred along both companies. For example, in 2003, the Indian state of Kerala revoked PepsiCo's water usage license and declined to renew Coca-Cola's. Since then, both companies have implemented supply-chain water-management programs, including partnering with government organizations (e.g., USAID), environmental NGOs (e.g., WWF and The Nature Conservancy), and local communities in developing countries to promote watershed management, improve water supply, sanitation, and hygiene, and enhance the efficiency of water use in production. Coca-Cola, for example, has committed to assessing the risks and vulnerabilities of its water sources at each one of its more than 900 bottling plants. The company says it intends to implement a protection plan for "source water" at each plant.

Coca-Cola is aiming to improve the efficiency and effectiveness of its water management. At the same time, however, as with Hindustan Unilever's water-stewardship efforts, Coca-Cola's projects are providing the company with strategic knowledge for its primary goal: to maintain secure supplies of its most important industrial input. "As the main ingredient in our products and an important part of our manufacturing processes," Coca-Cola explains, "water is essential to the sustainability of our business."[11] PepsiCo emphasizes the same eco-business advantage with the title of its inaugural global water report: "Water Stewardship: Good for Business. Good for Society."[12] John Paterson, IBM's vice-president of global supply and chief procurement officer, sums up the corporate reasoning behind rolling out water sustainability across IBM's supply chains: "In the long term as the Earth's resources get consumed, prices are going to go up. We've already seen large price increases and problems with water. . . . It's clear that there [are] real financial benefits to be had for procurers across the world to get innovative with their suppliers."[13]

Among brewers, SABMiller, with global beer brands such as Miller, Grolsch, Peroni, and Pilsner Urquell, has been a leader in demonstrating financial returns from working closely with its suppliers. Calculating that more than 90 percent of its "water footprint" was not from bottling facilities but rather from the growing of wheat and barley crops, SABMiller reports that it has been engaging local farmers (in partnership with

The Nature Conservancy) to reduce local agricultural water consumption and improve crop management. The program, SABMiller claims, is improving water access and water quality for local residents *and* significantly reducing water treatment costs. For example, by educating Colombian farmers on what they say are "better management processes," and paying them to put in hedges and keep cattle off of steep slopes, SABMiller says it is helping to improve local water quality as well as realizing significant savings at its plant. The company claims that its program is reducing the costs of water treatment in the City of Bogotá, too.[14]

Coercing and Cooperating for Added Value

As was noted in chapter 3, big-brand companies now recognize a potential to grow by emphasizing the improved "sustainability" of their mainstream brand offerings. In particular, through eco-business strategies they are linking the concept of sustainability with quality and then using this to differentiate their products in order to drive increased sales. Nike has done this with high-performance shoes and sports jerseys made from recycled waste. Walmart, Costco, Kroger, Super Target, Safeway, Marks & Spencer, Carrefour, Tesco, and Aldi are among those that have invested heavily in private-label "Organics" products sold alongside conventional brands. They are also harnessing sustainability for even bigger mainstream sales by eliminating and replacing some unhealthy product ingredients in their leading brand products. For example, Frito-Lay (PepsiCo's snack food division) has promised to replace monosodium glutamate, chemical red dye, and other artificial ingredients with "all-natural" ingredients in half of its mainstream convenience foods, including Tostitos tortillas, Multigrain Sunchips, Rold Gold pretzels, and Lay's potato chips.

The eco-business incentive to infuse brands with sustainability attributes is, in turn, encouraging big brands to push greening goals up through their supply chains to improve supplier practices. They are achieving this partly through compliance-driven tools such as supplier codes of conduct, auditing, and certification and partly through more cooperative "shared value" approaches with suppliers. According to Frances Way, Program Director of the Carbon Disclosure Project, real commercial returns are encouraging cooperation here: "[W]hereas [in 2009] we saw a rise in the number of large organizations embedding climate-change policy into the business strategy, now these policies are increasingly being put into practice at an operational level, across the entire supply chain. . . . Suppliers and large purchasing corporations alike are starting to realize the commercial benefits as a result of collaboration."[15] The example of the cocoa supply-chain initiatives of Mars, Hershey, Kraft, and Nestlé is illustrative. Efforts to cooperate in the coffee sector are also revealing.

In 2010, Nestlé (the world's largest food company, with the largest coffee brand) introduced the Nescafé Plan, a strategy for sustainable sourcing and production of its instant coffee. Partnering with the Rainforest Alliance and the Sustainable Agriculture Network, Nestlé agreed to invest $336 million over ten years in working with coffee farmers to implement its Nescafé Better Farming Practices, which include trying to use less water and chemicals and trying to avoid the clearing of rainforests. More fundamentally for Nestlé, the Nescafé Plan aims to improve the quality of coffee crops, and ultimately to increase Nestlé's supply of high-quality coffee beans.

Walmart is also helping to shift the "sustainable" coffee market (i.e., organic and fair trade) into the mainstream with its private-label Colombian coffee products. While working to build cooperative relations and improve practices with its suppliers, the company is also taking a strong-arm approach, making it clear to its suppliers that it will buy its coffee elsewhere if growers do not meet its quality and sustainability expectations. Suppliers "need to see that we're serious about directing our purchase decisions towards sustainable products," Walmart vice-president Steve Broughton explains, "and that with the right quality, farming, and business practices they will have a buying partner for their coffee."[16]

Big brands are gaining additional business value by working with suppliers to improve the efficiency and productivity of processing technologies and techniques while still keeping costs low. Although this buyer pressure can translate into poorer business practices and worker conditions if suppliers cut corners to try to find ways to cut costs, in at least some cases big-brand companies are providing suppliers with training and advice to help define and implement more responsible (yet still economical) practices. IKEA, for example, reports that it is working with seventy of its suppliers to reduce energy consumption and greenhouse gases and, through these efforts, to promote cost savings. One textile factory in Bangladesh, IKEA claims, reduced its energy consumption by 20 percent and its carbon dioxide emissions by 10,000 metric tons in the first six months of the project. By the end of the first year, that plant was projecting savings of €530,000 on an initial investment of €70,000. Similarly, IKEA reports that in the first year alone one of its Lithuanian suppliers of board material improved its energy efficiency by 37 percent and achieved savings of €350,000.[17]

Walmart has set its sights on improving the business performance of its small to medium-size suppliers by engaging in many small-scale eco-business projects around the world. By partnering with the World Environment Center on a Greening the Supply Chain program, for example, Walmart reports it was able to increase manufacturing output while at the same time reducing energy, water, oil, and waste costs among 19 food and beverage suppliers in Central America.

Walmart is claiming similar efficiency gains among suppliers in India. Bharti Walmart, since first forming in 2008, reports that it has reduced waste and sped up delivery times among its suppliers without compromising quality. A small anecdotal example is Haider Nagar, who supplies cucumbers to Walmart from his farm in the Punjab. He has increased his yields by 25 percent, he estimates, just by taking Walmart's advice. Walmart, he further claims, is paying 5–7 percent more than local wholesalers—and the company is picking up his cucumbers for free.[18] Walmart's CEO, Mike Duke, is using Walmart's position as the world's biggest grocery buyer to expand eco-business programs worldwide. "Our efforts," he claims, "will help increase farmer incomes, lead to more efficient use of pesticides, fertilizer and water, and provide fresher produce for our customers."[19] The efficiency gains will also help to keep prices low for Walmart's customers.

Rolling Back Prices

In July 2011, in the midst of a surge in commodity prices, IKEA announced an across-the-board price reduction of 2–3 percent for its 10,000 products, and promised to do the same again in 2012. Also in 2011, when many small retailers were increasing prices to cover higher costs and slower consumer demand, Walmart announced more than 100,000 "price rollbacks" at its Canadian stores. In 2012, Walmart topped this with a commitment to reduce grocery prices at all its US stores by $1 billion over the course of the year. Other big-brand retailers too are offering continual discounts in order to attract and keep customers.

Although many businesses are facing higher costs as commodity prices surge, big-brand buyers are more able to push costs back onto suppliers to avoid having to pass them on to "recession-strapped" consumers. "When our grocery suppliers bring price increases," explains Pamela Kohn, Walmart's general merchandise manager for perishables, "we don't just accept them."[20] Walmart and IKEA aim to keep their supply chains efficient so as to keep prices low. This aspect of the mass retail business model is crucial to upholding slogans such as IKEA's "Affordable Solutions for Better Living" and Walmart's "Save Money. Live Better."

Big brands know that their supply chains typically account for between 60 percent and 90 percent of their total costs.[21] With global market volatility and inflationary pressures increasing, controlling these costs is even more essential for all businesses now than it was in the past. As our previous examples have shown, big-brand companies are adopting eco-business to help increase supply-chain cost control by encouraging leaner supply chains. For the more responsible companies, this means cutting costs such as excess packaging, waste, and resource use. For others, though, it can mean cutting such expenses as labor benefits and quality controls.

Lean supply chains have greater efficiency and lower costs. Companies that focus solely on increasing production output per unit of resource inputs, however, may not be able to guarantee the best quality. Balancing high-volume productivity with quality is therefore an ongoing challenge. Eco-business within supply chains is striving to achieve both. Big brands are pushing suppliers to be more efficient while also demanding that they meet sustainability process and product requirements.

Suppliers, as we saw in chapter 4, often have little choice but to comply or risk losing a major buyer. Most don't even complain, in part because many sign contracts that demand silence—even anonymity—about purchasing deals. Trader Joe's standard supplier agreement, for example, requires that the "vendor shall not publicize its business relationship with TJ's in any manner."[22] Even without such a legal clause, few suppliers would dare challenge a buyer as big as Walmart, McDonald's, Procter & Gamble, or Nestlé. This is especially true for small subcontracted lower-tier suppliers in the developing world. But even General Mills, a multi-billion-dollar top-tier supplier company with Cheerios, Betty Crocker, and Pillsbury among its brands, may have to dance to a big retailer's tune. In 2010, Walmart accounted for 30 percent of General Mills' net sales in the United States.[23]

As was explained in chapter 2, big brands are maintaining their low-price advantage by outsourcing large quantities from the cheapest locations worldwide and using their economic might to keep the costs down. Many supply chains link into China. But these chains are also changing constantly. With rising wages and currency appreciation in China, the big brands are now looking to find even lower-cost suppliers elsewhere. In addition, as global shipping costs increase with rising energy prices, some companies are now looking for suppliers closer to home.

"Sustainable" Shipping

The global retail economy depends on cheap transportation of consumer goods by rail, truck, plane, and particularly by ship. More than 80 percent of global trade by weight involves sea travel. Running shoes, canned fruit, toothpaste, pillows, and laptop computers regularly cross oceans packed on wooden pallets in large steel containers on huge vessels. Since the shift to Chinese export manufacturing in the early 1990s, container shipping has been one of the world's fastest-growing sectors, with annual growth of about 10 percent. The numbers and the sizes of ocean-going ships continue to grow. In 2009, there were fifteen ships capable of carrying 10,000 20-foot containers. Two years later, there were more than sixty, with many more on order.[24] This market growth is concentrated among a few large trans-ocean shipping companies that wield power within retail supply chains that move products through a limited number of ports, canals, and vessels. The cost of shipping also continues to rise. For example, the cost of shipping a 40-foot container from Shanghai to the United States increased from about $3,000 in 2000 to $8,000 in 2008.[25]

To use less fuel and thus reduce carbon emissions, many carriers are now "slow steaming"—that is, reducing the speed of their ships. The US Federal Maritime Commission estimates that more than half of the ships traveling between Asia and the West Coast of the United States are slow steaming, as are more than three-fourths traveling between Asia and the East Coast. Maersk—named Shipping Operator of the Year in 2009 for implementing slow steaming—is reportedly saving 280 tons of fuel a day by reducing the speed of its largest ships.[26]

Carriers are struggling to keep costs down and winning awards for slow shipping. But unlike in many other areas, big-brand companies have less supply-chain control and are not necessarily seeing business gains. Matching supply cycles with demand cycles is crucial to controlling costs for big brands. Materials or finished goods that arrive too early or too late create extra costs. Longer transit times from slow steaming can also cause less reliable delivery schedules, which can tie up inventory and increase wait times for customers. This would be offset somewhat if the cost of shipping were going down, but it has been rising in recent years. In view of the financial benefit of slow steaming to the carriers, the US Federal Maritime Commission launched an inquiry in 2011 to investigate whether the carriers are unfairly colluding to keep prices high rather than pass on the savings. The commission is also implementing new monitoring rules to provide "unprecedented scrutiny" of decisions that affect American importers and exporters and continue to encourage reporting of "evidence of improper activities or collusion."[27]

To manage logistical challenges such as slow steaming and rising freight costs, and to try to gain influence over transportation, brand retailers, particularly in the grocery and apparel sectors, are working with ocean carriers through groups like the Business for Social Responsibility's Clean Cargo Working Group.[28] They are also aiming to gain more supply-chain power by increasing local sourcing and by "swimming upstream" (that is, cutting out supply-chain "middlemen" and manufacturing their own private-label products). This helps to reduce freight costs. It connects the retailers more directly to local suppliers, which, as explained earlier, can have productivity and quality benefits. And the big-brand companies also see it as a way to connect more directly with consumers to increase product sales.

Connecting with Consumers

"The retail supply chain is an extremely complex system," SAP consultants explain, "with an exceedingly simple goal: to fulfill consumer demand for goods."[29] Big brands are pursuing eco-business to not only enhance their power to dictate upstream costs and quality, but also to meet downstream consumers' demands to maintain revenue growth. Companies are employing eco-business to engage increasingly discerning consumers across all demographics, who are increasingly expecting brands to be value priced *and* responsible.

Big-brand companies by nature focus on the customer. Understanding and meeting consumers' needs, however, seems to be more important than ever. In a book titled *How Companies Win*, business pundits Rick Cash and David Kalhoun show that corporations must now focus more on the demand side of production chains to remain competitive. "The supply chain takes costs out," they argue. "The demand chain puts profits in. It's the business model of the 21st century."[30] Long-established big brands know this well. They are successful precisely because they have built a relationship of trust with consumers. But with new consumers, social media, and shifting consumer expectations, this relationship is changing. Different, more personalized marketing and sales strategies are required, and big brands are using eco-business to stimulate innovation.[31]

Multi-Channel Eco-Business

Although poorly understood and defined, the idea of sustainability is resonating more and more with consumers. Although their purchase decisions do not yet reflect their increasingly stated interest and concern, big-brand companies anticipate a growing demand. This is particularly true for the "millennial generation" (those born between the mid 1970s and 2000). For marketers, this is a fragmented and difficult-to-reach generation, with about 80 million members in the United States alone. It is also the next big wave of consumers, and the generation most likely, surveys predict, to integrate concern for the planet into purchase decisions.[32]

Consumers overall are now "more restrained, less trusting," and are "increasingly redefining what they value," consultants at A. T. Kearney explain.[33] Through online retail channels and through social media, consumers are engaging more in product offerings and looking to gain more influence over what goes onto retail shelves. "Crowdsourcing," in which consumers take part in designing their own products, is a growing expectation, particularly among the millennial generation.

No doubt mass marketing with a single message continues to shape consumers' preferences and choices. Yet big brands are finding value in using personalized promotions to meet the precise needs of consumers. Three-fourths of the companies in North America now have in place a process for contacting customers to request feedback on their firms and brands.[34] "Flogging"—fake blogging, with scripted entries written by company representatives—is occurring, too. In many cases, however, the new-media efforts seem genuine, with the big brands both accepting compliments and allowing criticisms in open online forums as part of their efforts to learn, shape perceptions, and win over consumers. When SC Johnson launched its new Windex mini-refill pouches, which use 90 percent less plastic packaging than their predecessors, the company's senior vice-president of global corporate affairs, communication, and sustainability, Kelly Semrau, said: "We want to create an open dialogue and get feedback from consumers. . . . We know this initial test won't be perfect, but to create real change we need to hear what consumers want and need, and learn as we go."[35] Her use of language here is revealing in that it emphasizes the company's drive for "real change" and deflects criticism with the acknowledgment that it is far from perfect. To gain acceptance, many big brands are positioning their eco-business efforts with consumers in a similar way.

Big-brand companies, as has already been noted, are using the social media to engage consumers. They are also adopting eco-business strategies to redesign their "brick-and-mortar" retail outlets to improve how they reach consumers. The "big-box" formula of stocking 100,000 or so different products so as to encourage one-stop shopping, although a lightning rod for criticism, remains a lucrative business model. Some big brands are even expanding their "boxes." IKEA, for example, plans to triple the size of its outlet in Oslo. Nonetheless, to better connect with all demographic groups (including those in emerging economies), and with the growing number of shoppers expecting the conveniences of online shopping, many big-box retailers are experimenting with smaller stores located closer to urban centers.

Tesco already operates many small "Fresh and Easy Market" outlets. The German discount grocery chain Aldi—the world's ninth-largest food retailer—is another market leader in smaller-format convenience retail. Many of the big brands, including Best Buy, The Office Depot, Staples, Gap, Toys "Я" Us, and Walmart, are following suit. Walmart has plans to open hundreds of small-format stores (one-third to one-tenth the size of its typical 150,000-square-foot superstore) across the United States under new banners such as "Walmart Express," "Walmart Market," and "Walmart on Campus."

Big brands are using what they describe as "small, simple retail formats" to project an image of sustainability that can reduce the backlash against warehouse-size outlets with stadium-size parking lots. The new model, they argue, can create a "neighborhood feel." In addition, they are emphasizing that customers do not have to drive as far, thus saving money and putting less stress on the environment.

These smaller stores are helping companies to expand their markets in previously inaccessible yet highly coveted urban locations. Walmart, Supervalu, and Walgreens, for example, are opening small-format stores in new locations in cities across the United States with the support of First Lady Michelle Obama, who is advocating for more affordable healthy food options in urban "food deserts."

Scaling Up Eco-Business

The reach of eco-business, then, is accelerating in large part because more big brands now recognize its value for improving the performance of supply chains. This is helping them to enhance their control over resource supplies, product quality, reliability, manufacturing, and delivery costs, as well as the prices of the hundreds of thousands of branded products that flow through global supply chains and onto retail shelves—a control that is more essential than ever for gaining a competitive advantage and sustaining growth in today's global economy. Fundamentally, big brands are adopting eco-business to enhance their power to get the right product to the right customer at the right time, place, and price with the most efficient use of resources, in order to sustain their retail power.

The rising power of big brands within globalizing supply chains is, in turn, strengthening the reach and influence of their eco-business efforts. Everywhere, politicians and activists are now seeking to partner with these global powerhouses. Getting Walmart on board can be a real victory for those wanting to see change happen quickly and with measurable global impact. "The capacity of Walmart to change the nutritional content of food in the US rivals that of the US Food and Drug Administration," said Michael Jacobson, executive director of the Center for Science in the Public Interest (a Washington-based consumer advocacy group) about Walmart's decisions in 2010 to reduce the prices of healthy foods in its US stores and to press suppliers to reduce sodium, sugar, and trans fats in packaged products. Walmart, Michelle Obama said, has "the potential to transform the marketplace and help Americans put healthier foods on their tables every single day."[36]

Walmart's decision, like other eco-business efforts, could well do some good. It is hard to imagine a more direct way to change the buying and eating patterns of middle-income and lower-income American families. Yet, although big-brand eco-business as a governance lever for change offers some prospects, it also has significant limits and many worrisome consequences.

6

Eco-Business Governance

Eco-business is not turning big brands into sustainable companies. Nor will it solve the world's environmental problems. As corporate executives readily admit, they are in the business of selling more products and are a long way from meeting their "aspirational" goals for sustainability. Walmart is not, in the words of business pundits Aron Cramer and Zachary Karabell, turning into "the unlikely epicenter of sustainable excellence"—at least not in terms of enhancing the ecological integrity of the earth itself. Yet the governance power of these companies to shape production and consumption decisions worldwide is unprecedented and enticing to attempt to harness. Already, as Cramer and Karabell note, many analysts see them as having "more influence on the business environment than the US government and other regulators."[1]

As we saw in chapter 2, growing and concentrating retail markets are one source of big brands' increasing influence. But eco-business is another. As we saw in chapters 3–5, big-brand companies are using sustainability for market advantage, framing it in corporate terms to gain greater efficiencies, supply-chain control, and brand growth. Eco-business is also reinforcing the credibility of big-brand companies to keep growing as well as govern other companies. Through strategic eco-business collaboration with industry, non-governmental organizations, governments, and consumers, big brands are positioning and achieving recognition as credible "sustainability leaders"—enhancing, we argue, their corporate reputations, power, and acceptance as governors of sustainability and global business.

One important source of the legitimizing power of eco-business is its capacity to go beyond rhetoric to produce some measurable improvements in environmental management. Although far from perfect, big brands are extending programs to manage waste, energy, water, and materials throughout their global operations in ways we have never seen before. Seeing this potential, many governments and activist groups are hoping to harness these programs to ratchet up business standards to move past the political stalemates and weak formal mechanisms that now characterize global environmental governance. "Our goal in working with Walmart," the Environmental Defense Fund states, "is to leverage what the retailer does best—creating efficient systems, driving change down through its supply chain and accessing a huge customer base—in order to dramatically advance environmental progress."[2] Former Vice-President Al Gore also sees big brands as having a crucial role in reducing the impact of consumers on the global environment. "[A] surprising amount of real progress is taking place," he asserts in a 2011 article in *Rolling Stone,* and consumers ought to make choices that "reward those companies that are providing leadership."[3]

Such praise is reinforcing the big brands' takeover of sustainability. Most activists know this. An industry-framed sustainability agenda and approach is obviously partial to market interests. And most would see strong public engagement and regulatory approaches to sustainability as necessary. Yet many activists also now see business as an essential part of shaping any sustainability solution, with regulating and campaigning against big brands going only part way toward improving business practices, particularly on a global scale. This explains why so many advocacy groups and state agencies are now partnering with big brands despite the obvious risks: they want access to the unparalleled private governance power.

Big Brands' Governing Authority

Eco-business improvements in brand company practices and products are adding legitimacy to big-brand leadership. This *does not* mean, however, that these companies are obtaining blind acceptance of the value of these improvements. Many governments and advocacy groups, for example, question the results of eco-business, emphasizing that what may look like a "gain" may be temporary, may involve hidden or unknown ecological and social costs, or may primarily reflect how a company is defining and calculating terms. Many analysts also struggle with (but often sidestep) an even more fundamental challenge: any so-called gain has to be assessed within the context of its absolute contribution to rising consumption and overall cumulative environmental pressures.[4]

Most are well aware that gains are small relative to total problems; still, many see a potential to nudge some of the gains along. Also, at least according to corporate definitions and measures, many of these gains do seem to have some merit. In the year 2010 alone, the US department store Kohl's, for example, bought enough "green power" (1.4 billion kilowatt-hours) to meet 100 percent of its purchased electricity use; the Swedish retailer H&M used 15,000 tons of organic cotton, more than three times its targeted amount (moving it to the top spot as the world's largest buyer of organic cotton); Tesco and Unilever in the UK diverted 100 percent of their waste from landfills; and Best Buy reported that it had recycled more than 70,000 tons of appliances and electronics, up from 30,000 tons in 2007 (working toward its goal of diverting 500,000 tons by 2015). So, although not by any means a global environmental solution, and while far from the potential scale that these companies could achieve, big-brand companies are demonstrating what appear to be some measurable gains that are lending them legitimacy and thus governance authority (i.e., legitimate power, not just buyer influence) to lead.[5] Even greater credibility gains, though, are arising from eco-business partnerships.

Jockeying for Cooperation

Big-brand companies have recognized that their competitiveness increasingly hinges on cooperation. The big brands are not alone in their thinking here. Joseph Nye, in his 2011 book *The Future of Power*, captures well the importance of building cooperative trust to retain global power in the twenty-first century: "It is not enough to think of power *over* others. We must also think in terms of power to accomplish goals that involves power *with* others. . . . In this world, networks and connectedness become an important source of relevant power."[6] Big-brand CEOs see the same need to connect and build networks to legitimize their influence. "We can't do it alone," says Nike's CEO, Mark Parker. "We need partners. We need collaboration from industry, civil society and government."[7] Through eco-business, they are now pursuing collaborative alliances, not just with suppliers and customers, but also with competitors, governments, advocacy organizations, consumers, and local communities.

With eco-business goals now linked to competitive positioning and brand reputation, failure has become a more costly option for big brands. To avoid this, as we saw in chapters 4 and 5, rather than confining efforts to their own operations and stopping after achieving relatively easy cost savings, many big-brand companies are looking further to drive eco-business through their supply chains. In addition, they are jockeying for position within a growing number of company-led sustainability bodies, including industry-association working groups and new cross-sector consortia that claim to promote corporate responsibility. And this is on top of participation in multi-stakeholder sustainability projects and private standard-setting bodies.

Big brands are cooperating to help them get over hurdles and move more efficiently toward eco-business targets. Industry-wide efforts can help keep the playing field level to protect their competitive position. Critics see the drive to "cooperate for sustainability" as, among other things, a veil behind which big-brand companies are able to collude and gain market power. For example, as was mentioned in chapter 1, in 2011 the European Commission fined Unilever and Procter & Gamble more than $450 million for breaching competition law by unfairly cooperating to set prices when introducing eco-friendly laundry detergents. Distinguishing the boundary between "pre-competitive" sustainability cooperation and monopolistic behavior is a growing issue, as the WWF's vice-president Jason Clay has written.[8] The big-brand companies, however, are claiming that these cooperative cross-sector and industry association initiatives are scaling up eco-business within supply chains, demonstrating their "leadership" on global sustainability.

Lobbying for Policy Leadership

The World Business Council for Sustainable Development, the International Business Leaders Forum, Business for Social Responsibility, Ceres, and other business organizations continue to work with companies, including the big brands, to promote and advance corporate efforts to position themselves on sustainability issues. For the most part, these groups acted independently since forming in the late 1980s and the early 1990s. Recently, however, the picture has become more complicated and cooperative as new groups have been formed and as mainstream business organizations, such as trade associations, have embraced similar corporate sustainability agendas.

Tens of thousands of trade associations around the world serve to facilitate standardization and cooperation among companies, as well as to lobby governments on behalf of members for less restrictive markets and less prescriptive standards. This lobbying certainly continues. To some extent, however, big-brand companies are also employing new strategies. In one high-profile case, Nike withdrew from the world's largest business lobbying organization—the US Chamber of Commerce—because of the Chamber's opposition to climate-change legislation. Nike's press release portrayed the move as an effort to take a more proactive and practical position: "Nike believes that climate change is an urgent issue affecting the world today and that businesses and their representative associations need to take an active role to invest in sustainable business practices and innovative solutions to address the issue. It is not a time for debate but instead a time for action and we believe the Chamber's recent petition sets back important work currently being undertaken by the EPA on this issue."[9]

After withdrawing from the US Chamber of Commerce, Nike formed a new organization with Levi Strauss & Co., Starbucks, and Timberland: Business for Innovative Climate and Energy Policy. Other big-brand companies, including Gap, Best Buy, Target, and eBay, have subsequently joined the group. Their declared goal is to lobby *for*, rather than against, US climate-change policy, aiming for more corporate input into its shaping. This has not deterred the US Chamber of Commerce from lobbying against climate legislation. Nor has it stopped other industry associations and big brands from continuing to push back against many new laws, as the lobbying against the "conflict minerals" provisions of the Dodd-Frank Act in 2010 demonstrates. Nonetheless, for image-building and strategic reasons, more and more industry associations are beginning to encourage members to position themselves as "pro-sustainability" in regard to energy, water, and waste. And in July of 2011 the US Chamber of Commerce, under the auspices of the Business Civic Leadership Center, held its first-ever conference on corporate sustainability.

With big brands in leadership roles, many retail and manufacturing trade associations are establishing working groups on sustainability. In 2007, the two biggest US retail associations—the National Retail Federation (the world's largest retail association) and the Retail Industry Leaders Association (formerly the Mass Retailing Institute)—both adopted corporate sustainability as a strategic focus. The Retail Industry Leaders Association now aims to ensure that members are "recognized by customers and policymakers for leadership in environmental stewardship." And the National Retail Federation has set up a Sustainable Retailing Consortium with nine "working councils" to monitor and encourage recycling, packaging reduction, green buildings, renewable energy, and supply-chain responsibility.

Trade associations are, no doubt, using sustainability programs to counter the potential for state legislators or NGOs to set a higher performance bar.[10] Still, a growing number are aiming to improve and better communicate the eco-business practices of members. This includes delivering sustainability education and training; developing sector-wide performance measures, benchmarks, and codes of conduct; and tracking progress. It also includes sharing new eco-business tools, such as the National Retail Federation's carbon footprint and sustainability scorecard for suppliers.

Industry associations are also increasingly seeing transparency and accountability as strategic goals. This includes encouraging members to participate in global cross-sector initiatives, such as Global Compact LEAD, the Global Reporting Initiative, the Dow Jones Sustainability Index, and the Carbon, Water, and Forest Footprint Disclosure Projects. In addition, for the first time, many associations are preparing sustainability summary reports highlighting innovation, and documenting overall industry sector progress, shortfalls, and challenges.

The British Retail Consortium, for example, launched an initiative in 2008 called "A Better Retailing Climate" that calls for members—including Tesco, Boots, Marks & Spencer, Homebase, and WHSmith—not only to pursue long-term sustainability goals, but also to report annually on progress toward them. This reporting is providing statistical backing for sustainability claims and leadership positioning. The Consortium's 2010 report claims that the major retailers had collectively reduced the amount of waste sent to landfill by 50 percent as well as cut energy use in their buildings and transport systems by 17 percent and 12 percent respectively (relative to 2005 levels).[11] The report also mentions some of the ongoing challenges of tackling rising absolute consumption impacts (e.g., increasing total fuel usage) as well as institutional and structural barriers to future progress, such as inadequate government coordination, labor skills, recycling infrastructure, and consumer education.

Industry association efforts to publicize corporate sustainability leadership through greater sector-wide transparency continue to increase. For instance, a 2010 report by the US Grocery Manufacturers Association, *Reducing Our Footprint*, highlights the efforts of its more than 300 members—including McDonald's, Kraft, Procter & Gamble, and Safeway—to avoid 4 billion pounds of packaging by 2020 by reducing, reusing, and recycling. Among the growing number of examples of industry participation, the US Consumer Electronics Association also now reports (since 2008) on the environmental and social progress of its sector, emphasizing the best practices of such member companies as Apple, Philips, Dell, Panasonic, Sony, Hewlett-Packard, Microsoft, and Best Buy. Significantly, this association now covers supply chains—from product design to facilities, packaging, transportation, and customer use.[12]

New Big-Brand Consortia

Beyond positioning themselves as sustainability leaders through industry associations, big-brand companies are forming new sustainability organizations that focus on scaling up eco-business across industry sectors, particularly through global supply chains. (See table 6.1.)

Retailers and manufacturers formed the Consumer Goods Forum to develop and encourage environmental, social, and economic responsibility standards along consumer goods supply chains. Co-chaired by Coca-Cola and Carrefour, and with the CEOs of Tesco and Unilever heading its sustainability program, the Consumer Goods Forum announced at the 2010 Cancun Climate Summit a collective commitment of its 650 members to achieve zero deforestation by 2020. Publicly, Tesco CEO Sir Terry Leahy and Unilever CEO Paul Polman emphasized the importance of sourcing sustainably: "We believe that our industry has a responsibility to purchase these commodities in a way which encourages producers not to expand into forested areas. Our task is to develop specific action plans for the different challenges of sourcing commodities like soya, palm oil, beef, paper and board sustainably."[13] Other sub-groups of the Consumer Goods Forum, such as the Global Packaging Project chaired by Kraft and Tesco, are taking a similar approach.

Table 6.1
The rise of big-brand corporate sustainability consortia.

Consortium	Year formed	Stated purpose
Sustainable Apparel Coalition	2011	Encourage sustainable manufacturing and inform consumers of the ecological impact of clothing.
Consumer Goods Forum	2009	Develop and promote the implementation of responsibility standards along consumer goods supply chains.
The Sustainability Consortium	2009	Encourage more sustainable products through scientific research, innovative technology, and standards.
The Green Grid	2007	Improve the resource efficiency of data centers and computing systems.
Beverage Industry Environmental Roundtable	2006	Define a common framework and drive continuous improvement in beverage industry environmental stewardship.
Electronics Industry Citizenship Coalition	2004	Improve working and environmental conditions in electronics supply chains.

Other sectors are pursuing parallel strategies. Apple, Hewlett-Packard, Dell, Sony, and IBM are active members of the Electronic Industry Citizenship Coalition, established in 2004 to watch over electronics supply chains. The coalition has since developed a code of conduct and a carbon reporting system for suppliers. And it is working on initiatives like the Conflict-Free Smelter Program, which helps companies to identify the sources of higher-risk materials. The agri-food industry, meanwhile, formed the Sustainable Agriculture Initiative (one of the earliest consortia) in 2002 to monitor global food chains. With Nestlé, Unilever, and Danone among its members, it is defining and creating standards for "sustainable agriculture production," convening conferences, and supporting pilot projects involving farmers.

More recently, Nike and other big brands launched the Sustainable Apparel Coalition in 2011. Nike first took a leading role in organizing sustainability collaborations in 2008, when it became chair of the World Economic Forum's Consumer Industries Working Group on Sustainable Consumption. Nike proclaims that its goal as chair of that group is "to galvanize industry collaboration on solutions that will fast track the transition to a sustainable economy."[14]

Big brands, then, are positioning themselves as sustainability leaders through participation in industry associations and in new "sustainable business" consortia. This is helping big-brand companies to shape and agree on sustainability definitions and agendas that will advance their goals and reputations. To maintain (and increase) societal and political support to operate and grow, they are also increasingly collaborating on eco-business efforts with governments and NGOs.

Leading and Guiding Business

In the absence of consistent definitions of sustainability, big brands are stepping in to define a "sustainability vision" for business. The results in all cases call for greater cooperation, which is helping to position big-brand companies as team players seeking collective solutions: a successful formula for building support. "The level of business action," Neville Isdell of Coca-Cola tells us, "needs to move from 'incremental' steps in isolation to 'step-change' in collaboration."[15] Many are also adopting language more commonly heard within nonprofit organizations. A 2010 report by the World Economic Forum's Sustainability Initiative, which includes Best Buy, Kraft Foods, Nestlé, and Nike, states: "This is not about incremental improvements in the efficient use of particular inputs . . . it is about redefining value . . . it implies a transformation in the global economy . . . and it will be disruptive."[16] Other visioning projects, including the World Business Council for Sustainable Development's Vision 2050 and the World Economic Forum's Sustainable Consumption Initiative, are looking to explore pathways to what some are calling "sustainable prosperity" in a "green economy."

The efforts of big brands to guide and communicate a collective vision reveal some of the complex dynamics around eco-business. By leading brainstorming sessions and writing reports that try to imagine a path to a sustainable future, big-brand companies are building networks and governance cooperation among businesses, as well as with governments and NGOs. There are collective benefits here; but the companies clearly benefit, too. Visioning exercises are helping them shape the bounds of sustainability solutions and present a public image as responsible corporate citizens. These are also helping them to identify growth opportunities as well as to build acceptance for eco-business programs within global supply chains.

To some analysts, big-brand companies positioning themselves as sustainability "thought leaders" and "watchdogs" of any sort is paradoxical at best, and at worst devious and hypocritical—a corporate tactic to control the sustainability agenda. Others are more optimistic, though, seeing a potential here to encourage companies to do what they do best: innovate. Watchful, measured engagement will be important.

Partnering with NGOs

Twenty years ago, it was heresy for a non-governmental organization to consider partnering with a company. Corporations were "the enemy." Lines were drawn in the sand. Protest rallies and boycott campaigns were the norm. Likewise, corporations steered clear of activists, keeping them far away from the boardroom.

Now, although anti-corporate campaigns remain common (particularly through social media), partnerships are the norm more than the exception. A 2010 *Economist* survey found that "almost four-fifths (78%) of [business] respondents said that interaction with special interest groups, NGOs, or citizen groups is considered important to their business," and "this rises to 90% among companies in Western Europe."[17] And the trend toward working together continues. In 2009, Greenpeace and Coca-Cola announced that they would cooperate on at least some climate-change issues. In 2010, the world's largest environmental NGO (the WWF) and the world's largest consumer-goods company (Procter & Gamble) signed a three-year partnership agreement to try to improve energy, water, conservation, and sustainable sourcing of materials along Procter & Gamble's global supply chain.

NGOs, on the one hand, partner with companies such as Coca-Cola and Procter & Gamble, in the words of the head of Greenpeace UK, to get out of the "green ghetto" and access the power of corporations for swift, large-scale change.[18] Some NGOs accept financial compensation. Conservation International has many partnerships with financial commitments, some with big companies (including Walmart and Starbucks) and some with small ones (such as Fiji Water), although corporate financing is still only a small portion of Conservation International's total revenues (e.g., only 5 percent in 2007).

Companies, on the other hand, partner in order to gain a better understanding of the issues, to gain support for strategies, and, most important, to realize business gains by improving brand trust and reputation. Clorox's partnership with the Sierra Club helped Clorox capture more than 40 percent of the market for natural cleaning products with its new Green Works products carrying the Sierra Club logo. In return, the Sierra Club helped millions of consumers get more affordable access to more sustainable household products. It also received a check for a percentage of Clorox's first-year sales of the new products.[19]

Maintaining independence from NGO partners is important to corporations too. If they lose this impartiality, they can lose much of the credibility the partnership is granting to eco-business. Avrim Lazar, President and CEO of the Forest Products Association of Canada, explains: "Environmental organizations translate your progress into recognition. Your company gets little recognition for its sustainability efforts until you've partnered with advocacy groups. They have the power to say what is or isn't 'green.'"[20]

Partnerships, although increasingly common, remain controversial, even within partner organizations. They do not guarantee a company unconditional support from an NGO. Many in the environmental community disagree as to whether partnering is advancing sustainability or compromising more transformational change. And views can differ sharply among supporters of an NGO like Greenpeace, which has historically spurned corporate collaboration.

The corporate world is divided, too. Advocates highlight the benefits of having NGOs in-house: to learn, keep an eye on them, and reduce the risk of being blindsided. Critics worry that partnerships put the corporation in a position of accountability to an unaccountable body. NGOs are not elected bodies, nor are they shareholders. Even within successful partnerships, the relationship can be one of both friend and foe. Greenpeace, for example, partnered with Unilever to develop eco-friendly

"Greenfreeze" for refrigerators. This did not stop them though from publicly criticizing and campaigning against Unilever on other issues. Greenpeace has a similarly multifaceted relationship with Nestlé. For many decades Greenpeace has been a tough critic of Nestlé, yet in 2011 it praised Nestlé's efforts to reduce the consequences of its purchasing practices for tropical deforestation. Greenpeace's senior climate adviser, Charlie Kronick, sees such pragmatism as essential for effective campaigning. "No NGO," he emphasizes, "remains a permanent friend or has a fixed position with regard to a company like Nestlé."[21]

Still, big brands are seeking NGOs—at times even more than governments—to help them deliver on eco-business goals. Unilever, for example, turned to the WWF, and not the International Maritime Association or the UN Law of the Sea secretariat, to address concerns about its frozen seafood supply and the need to tackle depleting fish stocks. Similarly, when Walmart was looking for assistance to "green" its supply chain for business value, it didn't go to the US Environmental Protection Agency. It turned to the WWF, the Environmental Defense Fund, and Green Seal.[22] Corporations and NGOs are cooperating because they realize they can be powerful allies in advancing some environmental and many business gains faster and even, in some cases, more extensively than government processes. Big brands recognize that they also need consumer trust and government endorsement, however, to fully legitimize their governance power.

Consumers and Reputational Legitimacy

Big brands have many incentives to communicate what they hear governments and NGOs telling them is "the right sustainability message." This helps them to influence consumer perceptions, counter backlash, protect their reputations, and sell more products. Tesco CEO Sir Terry Leahy, for example, announced at a Forum for the Future event in 2007 in London that the company would spend almost $1 billion over the next five years to lead "a revolution in green consumption," would label its products to reveal eco-footprints, and would help to establish a Sustainable Consumption Institute at the University of Manchester. For "Black Friday" (the day after Thanksgiving) 2011, Patagonia—as part of a "Common Threads" program that the company claims is aimed at convincing consumers to buy only what is necessary—took out a full-page ad in the *New York Times* telling shoppers *not* to buy its jacket. Ultimately, as Patagonia admits, this eco-business initiative proved profitable, attracting more discerning shoppers away from rival brands. "We don't think that telling people to buy less affects sales," said Patagonia's vice-president of global marketing. "If anything, it's increased them."[23]

Some companies are doing a better job than others of marketing eco-business efforts and winning support. Interbrand's ranking of "green brands," for example, found that L'Oreal, Nokia, and Hewlett-Packard are under-communicating their greening efforts, whereas consumers' perceptions of the sustainability efforts of McDonald's, General Electric, Coca-Cola, IKEA, and Starbucks exceed their actual performance.

The method and nature of communication is a strategic decision. Big brands recognize that sustainability claims and programs can either gain them or lose them the loyalty and trust of consumers. Edelman's 2011 "trust barometer" survey found that 73 percent of the consumers surveyed would refuse to buy products or services from a company they didn't trust.[24] Eco-business gains and more effective communication strategies have helped Nike and Walmart to repair damaged reputations. Nike's reputation has come a long way since it suffered from a torrent of bad publicity after *Life* magazine featured, on the cover of its June 1996 issue, a photo of a 12-year-old Pakistani boy playing with a Nike soccer ball, one of many he was being paid 60 cents a day to stitch.

Before 2005, Walmart was attracting some of the heaviest criticism, particularly for its labor practices and its impacts on local businesses. Integrating eco-business into its brand since then certainly hasn't deflected all criticism; however, it has improved Walmart's image, gaining it, to the confusion of many, a reputation as both the best and the worst sustainability performer. Edward Hume's 2011 book on Walmart tells the "unlikely story" of the company's "green revolution."[25] Now the company wins top rankings and awards, occupying (at least for a time) the top position among household consumer-products companies in the Carbon Disclosure Project's ranking and winning a Green Power Leadership award from the US Environmental Protection Agency.

Green consumerism is a complex prospect. Most consumers still make purchases on the basis of price and quality, even though most also state a preference for "sustainable products."[26] Recognizing that consumers are increasingly interested in corporate reputation and sustainability traits but don't want to pay more for "responsible" brands, companies are implementing various strategies to price "green" products the same as mainstream products.

At the same time, many brands continue to exaggerate sustainability claims. Unspecified labels like "all natural," "green," and "eco-friendly" are common, as is the use of "greenwash" tactics to make products "look" sustainable (for example, by putting them in dull brown packages rather than bright glossy ones, or by reducing the amount of product in each package). Still, the TerraChoice annual surveys have found that legitimate sustainability claims are increasing. For example, leading brands are participating in eco-certification organizations and labeling products with third-party independent "green seals of approval" rather than just "self-declaring" through their own private eco-logos. Not only is this enhancing brands' credibility among consumers; it is also making them more credible to governments.

Co-Regulatory Endorsement

In the last few decades, governments worldwide have turned to market-based policies that promote industry self-regulation. This has created an enabling environment for eco-business. Governments certainly have the power to thwart eco-business though. Those who fear that the rise of eco-business governance will lead to a complete corporate takeover of sustainability favor this course of action—that is, to "bring the state back" and re-embed sustainability in the public realm. Government monitoring and regulations are certainly required to stop companies from colluding or misleading consumers. But opportunities exist as well for governments to encourage, assist—and even *adopt* alongside state operations—eco-business governance tools.

Recently, governments are doing more to endorse and lend credibility to big-brand governance. The US Environmental Protection Agency, for example, praised Walmart in 2011 for its effort to step ahead of federal regulators to ban polybrominated diphenyl ethers (flame retardants) from its products and, in the absence of regulations, to do its own testing to enforce its policy. "The EPA has long had concerns about PBDEs," notes the EPA's Steve Owens. "Walmart has taken an important step toward protecting children and families from exposure to toxic chemicals."[27]

Some state agencies are engaging eco-business through what policy scholars and practitioners (particularly in Europe) refer to as co-regulation—that is, public-private collaborative governance involving corporations and governments, and sometimes

NGOs. Some governments are going even further and incorporating voluntary corporate standards into public policy. Some governments in North America and Europe, for example, are mandating private forest certification on public forestlands to improve the market and societal acceptance of state forest management. Some are incorporating private eco-certification standards, such as the LEED green building standard, into public procurement requirements. Governments are not just enabling but also collaborating with big-brand eco-business. The US Conference of Mayors, for example, is cooperating with Walmart to help American cities reduce energy consumption and carbon emissions through a nationwide awards program.

Governments in emerging and developing economies are also leveraging eco-business to supplement domestic governance capacity and drive business innovation. The Yunnan provincial government in China, for example, signed an agreement with Starbucks that requires the company to help improve coffee-growing practices among local farmers. China's central government has also signed agreements with Walmart to require the company to roll out its corporate sustainability policies and programs across China's domestic retail, manufacturing, and resource-extraction sectors.[28]

Across an increasing number of jurisdictions, then, governments are seeing opportunities to harness the resources and eco-business tools of big-brand companies (e.g., life-cycle assessments, supplier scorecards, eco-label and certification criteria, audits, and reporting) to advance policy rules and goals, shape business practices, and supplement enforcement. (See table 6.2.) Many analysts see a potential for economic gains, such as improving the efficiency, quality, innovation, and global competitiveness of local companies. Many others see a need for big companies to step up and "govern" for global sustainability. "We need business leaders that can go beyond their own interests and act as 'global statesmen' in building a sound global system," Jeffrey Sachs of the Earth Institute at Columbia University said in 2010.[29] CEOs are acknowledging these growing expectations. "Weak public governance," Neville Isdell of Coca-Cola explains, "harms both a country's people and its environment . . . business has opportunity and motive to change that by contributing to building better governance systems and public institutions . . . which are fundamental to sustainable social and economic development and therefore sustainable communities and business success."[30]

The rise of big brands as private governing authorities is corporatizing the global political arena. And this certainly raises important concerns for the protection of public goods. But alongside strong state regulatory programs, it brings potential too: notably, a rise in the capacity of global environmental governance to keep pace with the global economy.

Keeping Pace with the Global Economy

Economic growth continues to outpace the institutional response to global environmental problems. The next 40 years will see the human population reach 9–10 billion, with per capita consumption already very high in developed countries and rising quickly in many developing ones. Without any change in the economic growth trajectory, per capita energy needs alone are set to at least double in the next 40 years. Coordination and fair representation in the global arena is exceedingly difficult, and multilateral agreements remain weak. The World Business Council for Sustainable Development explains the limitations of global governance well: "[T]he governance and policy responses to manage this growth often happen in silos and are limited by short term, localized political pressures, and thus fall short of the level of commitment needed

Table 6.2
Engaging eco-business for policy innovation.

Policy function	Eco-business tools	Policy leverage
Rule making	Life-cycle assessment Supply-chain tracing	LCA and tracing identify hotspots where policy interventions (e.g., new rules or incentives) could produce the greatest improvements.
Implementation	Supplier scorecards Procurement standards	Supplier scorecards and procurement standards define environmental rules and requirements that could be adopted into regulations to raise the bar on global production and product design standards.
Enforcement	Auditing Reporting Eco-certification*	These tools identify corporate failings, improvements, and best practices that could aid policy makers to better regulate, facilitate, and reward corporate advances.

*Eco-certification contributes to all three policy functions.

to make significant progress."[31] Far more hard-hitting action is necessary to keep pace with the ever-rising consequences of the global economy.

The Speed and the Scale of Big-Brand Sustainability

"Business should not be waiting for governments," says Christiana Figueres, executive secretary of the UN Framework Convention on Climate Change, "but taking the lead and pulling governments along."[32] More and more, political leaders are calling on big companies to lead the world out of the fast-approaching crisis of climate change. Companies can act more quickly and across more jurisdictions than governments—and those looking for a solution to climate change know this.

Although fraught with limits, the rise of eco-business presents an opportunity to govern on a *global* scale at higher speeds. The supply chains of the world's largest consumer-goods companies offer strong leverage points to produce the geographic range, dynamic response, and coordination necessary for systemic global change. Any one of these multinational companies can send signals and issue orders that virtually overnight change production and supply networks worldwide—a nearly impossible feat for a government or civil society organization.

Andy Tait, senior campaign advisor for Greenpeace captures the potential of such power well when explaining Nestlé's policy (announced in April 2010) to reduce its deforestation footprint: "Nestlé's policy sends a very clear message to companies. . . . If you don't stop deforestation and protect peatlands, your days of supplying to global brands such as Nestlé are over."[33] A year later Greenpeace issued an enthusiastic news release full of praise for Nestlé. "The food giant took a giant step forwards by agreeing to a set of unprecedented commitments. . . . The company is making a serious attempt to raise the bar when it comes to corporate action against deforestation."[34]

Big brands can also push other big brands to change their practices. The biggest producer of packaged consumer goods in the world, Procter & Gamble, reportedly jumped in response to Walmart's announcement in 2007 that it would be increasing its sourcing of more energy-efficient goods that were packaged more "sustainably." To meet Walmart's new guidelines, Procter & Gamble raced to spend more than $100 million in just over a year to redesign its laundry detergent product and packaging.

In addition, big-brand companies are coming together to coordinate supply chains. In one example of increasing cross-national collaboration, Cadbury, Danone, Kraft, Mars,

Coca-Cola, Nestlé, PepsiCo, Unilever, and Procter & Gamble have joined a global supply-chain governance mechanism called AIM-PROGRESS that is defining and setting standards and benchmarks for sourcing practices and eco-efficient production systems globally. The AIM-PROGRESS initiative has the backing of the European Brands Association and the American Grocery Manufacturers Association, as well as a partnership with SEDEX (a multi-stakeholder nonprofit organization that hosts an open data-exchange on the ethical practices of suppliers). Collaborative initiatives like this one are serving to further enhance the credibility and capacity of big brands to frame the global sustainability agenda. At the same time, however, the rise of big-brand governance is providing opportunities for state and non-state actors to influence production and suppliers more globally. And to a certain extent, it is bringing global environmental governance closer to the mainstream consumer.

Global Consumption and the Mainstream Consumer

An ongoing challenge of global governance is the disconnect between those making decisions and those primarily impacted by them. To some extent, big brands are making the governance of global issues more accessible—although arguably not more equitable in terms of representation—through multi-stakeholder deliberative processes on sustainability. Consumers, for example, are gaining opportunities to connect more directly with their "favorite brands," and are "voting" for more responsible product offerings through their purchase decisions and also through social media.

Consumers' purchasing can be an important point of leverage. Eco-conscious shoppers are in some respects a privileged elite, however—a fraction of global society able to afford premiums for products labeled as more sustainable. In what Walmart refers to as the "democratizing of sustainability," big brands are trying to counter this limitation by arguing they are incorporating sustainability into mass-produced products that are affordable to most households. The idea is to "green" mainstream consumer goods, and not just high-end food, fashion, and furnishings. One example, among many, is the move by Kraft Foods in 2011 to reduce the water use, energy, and packaging for common low-end household brands such as Kraft Macaroni and Cheese, Jell-O, Oreos, and Ritz Crackers.

Big brands are also encouraging consumers to engage more by providing them with clearer supply-chain information on product labels. These include special bar codes that enable consumers to get details on a company's sustainability efforts. Many challenges remain here, as was outlined in chapter 4, including the complexity of collecting and standardizing this information into an understandable rating that captures the tradeoffs among green attributes (e.g., carbon, water, waste, and energy sustainability) and supply-chain and product life-cycle impacts.

This kind of green consumerism moves us along but not very far forward toward an ecological meaning of sustainability. Many so-called sustainable products continue to contain questionable materials and continue to be designed for rapid obsolescence and disposal; and many consumers, in the words of George Monbiot, simply "rebrand their lives, congratulate themselves on going green, and carry on buying and flying as much as before."[35]

Ecological Sustainability

"Ours is a strategy of seeking major improvements, but not perfection," the Sierra Club says in justifying its partnerships with companies like Clorox.[36] But is this strategy helping? Is it making matters worse? As this book reveals, big brands *are* making big promises, positioning themselves as sustainability leaders, and even, when failing to meet targets, still working hard to seek out bottlenecks to boost efficiency. But is sustainability in any meaningful sense even possible within a world economy that relies on mass retail and growing consumerism?

Efficiencies are being realized. It now takes a smaller amount of natural resources to produce each dollar of economic growth—26 percent less in 2007 in comparison to 1980 levels, according to the Sustainable Europe Research Institute.[37] Nonetheless, gains are not keeping pace with economic growth, and *total* global ecological impacts keep rising. According to a 2011 World Economic Forum and Deloitte Touche Tohmatsu study of progress over the last few decades, "no absolute decoupling was achieved and resource extraction continues to grow in absolute terms."[38] The European Environment Agency's *State of the Environment Report* reaches similar conclusions: "[T]he pan-European region is generating ever more waste. . . . The intensification of economic activities outweighs the effects of waste prevention initiatives. . . . Energy consumption and resulting greenhouse gas emissions have also been increasing, despite energy efficiency improvements and an increased use of renewable energy in certain areas."[39]

Household consumption and per capita resource use continue to rise steadily in developed countries, and increase rapidly in emerging and developing economies. McKinsey consultants are projecting that over the next decade the spending of 2 billion middle-class consumers across a dozen emerging economies will increase from $6.9 trillion to $20 trillion (twice the United States' current consumption). In India alone, the *Business Monitor International* is predicting that between 2011 and 2015 retail sales will almost double, to about $800 billion.[40] And the world is watching closely as China attempts to rebalance and stabilize its economy by increasing domestic consumer spending.

If eco-business is accelerating, and if NGOs and governments are praising the successes of the big brands, why aren't things improving? Some emphasize the importance of a "rebound effect"—that is, as the efficiency of using a resource or making a product increases, the resulting savings are then directed toward more consumption, effectively canceling out the efficiency gains.[41] This is indeed occurring; but the problem, as growing numbers of people are aware, is even more fundamental. The rise of eco-business relies on—and indeed in some cases is driving—consumption trends that are overtaking the gains in speed, scale, and eco-efficiency. Incremental gains on a per-unit basis are not enough. Efficiencies and technological innovation in product and packaging design are not enough.

More and more governments and advocacy groups, as we have seen, are putting these fundamental concerns aside and trying to accelerate some of the possible pragmatic gains from eco-business. "Right now," Sally Uren of the NGO Forum for the Future says, "we need every weapon in our armoury to deal with the challenges we're facing. Whilst some puritans will be saying, '. . . brands, how can they ever save the world . . . they got us into this mess . . .' . . . we don't have time to get moral about this and question the integrity of using brands in this way. . . . Giving big brands like Unilever [and] PepsiCo wholescale sustainability makeovers might just give us the chance of meeting the scale of the challenges that we face."[42]

Engaging with Eco-Business

Whether activists or regulators like it or not, big brands are taking over sustainability and turning it into eco-business. This presents a great challenge for states and NGOs. Unheeded, this will continue to produce some limited gains: more efficiency, less packaging and waste per product, more eco-products, more solar panels and electric vehicles. But it will not get us even close to true sustainability—and it could well make things worse as big-brand discount consumerism surges and ecological shadows intensify. At the same time, as those rushing to partner are hoping, reorienting and leveraging eco-business might do some real good.

Any partner, however, needs to keep a sharp eye on the rhetoric and politics of eco-business and accept that it is fundamentally about business control and growth. It is about gaining legitimacy and projecting an image of responsibility. It is about increasing the transparency and accountability within supply chains to manage risks and extract profit. It is about securing increasingly scarce natural resources and competing for high-quality inputs. It is about raising the productivity of operations and suppliers. It is about gaining customers' trust. And it is about reducing costs, lowering consumer prices, and improving sales. In short, it is about sustaining business, not ecosystems. Consumer confidence has been low since the global financial downturn of 2007–2009, and companies need societal support to regain their footing. "It isn't good enough to just make the 'business case' for sustainability," business sustainability expert Peter Lacy explains. It is "also at a much more fundamental level, 'making the case for business.'"[43] Eco-business is doing both.

Those partnering to prod eco-business toward more far-reaching ecological and social goals face many dangers; some even risk capture and cooptation. The temptation to take such risks is certainly understandable, and, as we have seen, some opportunities do seem to exist to leverage eco-business for broader societal and ecological good. This has to be done, however, with great vigilance and tempered enthusiasm. As this book has shown, the motives and true goals of eco-business place strict limits on what it can—and ever will—achieve for the planet. But to simply ignore the efforts of big brands to take over sustainability and turn it into eco-business would ensure an even more perilous path into the future.

Notes

Chapter 1

1. See Nike's Corporate Responsibility Report FY07–09 homepage (http://www.nikebiz.com/crreport/).

2. We conflate big-box retailers and brand manufacturers into the term "big brands" because the eco-business of these companies is similar (and embedded in webs of corporate networks). Distinguishing between them is becoming increasingly problematic as Nike, Apple, Sony, and other manufacturers open retail stores and as Walmart, The Home Depot, and other retailers introduce private labels.

3. For the seminal article on strategic CSR, see Michael Porter and Mark Kramer "Strategy and Society: The Link Between Competitive Advantage and Corporate Social Responsibility," *Harvard Business Review* 84 (December) (2006), pp. 78–92. For recent literature, see Michael Porter and Mark Kramer, "Creating Shared Value," *Harvard Business Review* 89 (January–February) (2011), pp. 62–77; David Lubin and Daniel Esty, "The Sustainability Imperative," *Harvard Business Review* 88 (May) (2010), pp. 42–50; William Werther and David Chandler, *Strategic Corporate Social Responsibility: Stakeholders in a Global Environment* (Sage, 2010); David Baron, Maretno Harjoto, and Hoje Jo, *The Economics and Politics of Corporate Social Performance*, Research Paper No. 1993R, Stanford Graduate School of Business, 2009; Paul R. Portney, "The (Not So) New Corporate Social Responsibility: An Empirical Perspective," *Review of Environmental Economics and Policy* 2 (2) (2008), pp. 261–75; *Economist* Intelligence Unit, *Corporate Citizenship: Profiting from a Sustainable Business* (2008).

4. For analyses of "corporate sustainability" in the 1990s, see Michael Porter and Claas Van der Linde, "Green and Competitive: Ending the Stalemate," *Harvard Business Review* 73 (5) (1995), pp. 120–134; Stuart L. Hart and Gautam Ahuja, "Does It Pay to Be Green? An Empirical Examination of the Relationship Between Emission Reduction and Firm Performance," *Business Strategy and the Environment* 5 (1) (1996), pp. 30–37; Sanjay Sharma and Harrie Vredenburg, "Proactive Corporate Environmental Strategy and the Development of Competitively Valuable Organizational Capabilities," *Strategic Management Journal* 19 (8) (1998), pp. 729–753; John Elkington, *Cannibals with Forks: The Triple Bottom Line of 21st Century Business* (New Society, 1998); Simon Zadek, *The Civil Corporation: The New Economy of Corporate Citizenship* (Earthscan, 2001).

5. Stefan Schaltegger and Andreas Sturm were the first to publish the idea of eco-efficiency, in a 1989 WWZ Discussion Paper (no. 8914) with the main title Ökologieinduzierte Entscheidungsprobleme des Managements [Ecology-Induced Management Decision Support] (Basel, Switzerland: WWZ, Wirtschaftswissenschaftliche Fakultät Universtät Basel). Stephan Schmidheiny and the Business Council for Sustainable Development popularized this term in the 1992 MIT Press book *Changing Course: A Global Business Perspective on Development and the Environment.*

The MIT Press has been at the forefront of advancing the ideas and debates around eco-efficiency. See, for example, Stephan Schmidheiny and Federico J. L. Zorraquín (with the World Business Council for Sustainable Development), *Financing Change: The Financial Community, Eco-efficiency, and Sustainable Development* (1996); Livio DeSimone and Frank Popoff (with the World Business Council for Sustainable Development), *Eco-Efficiency: The Business Link to Sustainable Development* (1997); and the special issue on eco-efficiency of the *Journal of Industrial Ecology* (volume 9, number 4, 2005).

6. Jeffrey Immelt, "Global Environmental Challenges," speech at George Washington University, May 9, 2005.

7. "Future Friendly" is the name of Procter & Gamble's marketing campaign to educate mainstream consumers on its new line of more environmentally responsible products (e.g., cold-water detergent). Two recent examples of corporate visioning for "sustainable consumption" and "sustainable growth" are *Redesigning Business Value: A Roadmap for Sustainable Consumption* (Deloitte Touche Tohmatsu and World Economic Forum, 2010) and *The Consumption Dilemma:*

Leverage Points for Accelerating Sustainable Growth (Deloitte Touche Tohmatsu and World Economic Forum, 2011, updated April 2011).

8. Quoted on the website of the International Green Awards (http://www.greenawards.com).

9. See Nike's corporate website (http://www.nikebiz.com).

10. Quoted in Paul Rogers, "The Power of Green," *NYSE Magazine .com*, first quarter 2010 (available at http://www.nysemagazine.com).

11. Quoted in Boston Consulting Group, *Sustainability: The 'Embracers' Seize Advantage* (MIT Sloan Management Review Research Report, March 2011), p. 8.

12. A. Claire Cutler, "Private International Regimes and Interfirm Cooperation," in Peter Hall and Thomas Biersteker, eds., *Emergence of Private Authority in Global Governance* (Cambridge University Press, 2002), p. 24.

13. United Nations Economic Commission for Europe and Food and Agriculture Organization of the United Nations, *Forests Products Annual Market Review 2010–2011* (2011), pp. 99, 101.

14. Anne Roulin, Nestlé's head of packaging and design, made this estimate in March 2011. It is summarized in Dan Hockensmith, "Nestlé Targeting New Markets," *Plastic News* 22 (March 7, 2011), p. 3.

15. Hindustan Unilever, "Winning Today and Tomorrow," presentation to Investor Conference, May 10, 2011 (available at http://www.hul.co.in).

16. On the growing importance of corporate power in global environmental governance, see Peter Newell and Matthew Paterson, *Climate Capitalism: Global Warming and the Transformation of the Global Economy* (Cambridge University Press, 2010); Jennifer Clapp and Doris Fuchs, eds., *Corporate Power in Global Agrifood Governance* (MIT Press, 2009); Peter Utting and Jennifer Clapp, eds., *Corporate Accountability and Sustainable Development* (Oxford University Press, 2008); Matthew Paterson, *Automobile Politics: Ecology and Cultural Political Economy* (Cambridge University Press, 2007); Doris Fuchs, *Understanding Business Power in Global Governance* (Nomos, 2005).

17. Quoted in Simon Houpt, "Beyond the Bottle: Coke Trumpets Its Green Initiatives," *Globe and Mail*, January 13, 2011.

18. Greenpeace USA, "Market Solutions and Corporate Campaigning" (available at http://www.greenpeace.org).

19. Gwen Ruta, "20 Years of Business Partnership Lessons at EDF," interview recorded November 26, 2010 (available at http://sic.conversationsnetwork.org).

20. Quoted in Hans Schattle, "McDonald's Bids to Clean Up Its Reputation," *Boston Globe*, August 2, 1990.

21. Quoted in Alyson Genovese, "Engaging Success," Country Briefing: United States, *Ethical Corporation*, October 2010, p. 5.

22. For recent readings on the rise of business sustainability, see Edward Humes, *Force of Nature: The Unlikely Story of Wal-Mart's Green Revolution* (HarperCollins, 2011); Chris Laszlo and Nadya Zhexembayeva, *Embedded Sustainability: The Next Big Competitive Advantage* (Greenleaf, 2011); Aron Cramer and Z. Karabell, *Sustainable Excellence: The Future of Business in a Fast-Changing World* (Rodale, 2010); Daniel Esty and Andrew Winston, *Green to Gold: How Smart Companies Use Environmental Strategy to Innovate, Create Value, and Build Competitive Advantage*, second edition (Wiley, 2009); Joel Makower, *Strategies for the Green Economy: Opportunities and Challenges in the New World of Business* (McGraw-Hill, 2008); Adam Werbach, *Strategy for Sustainability: A Business Manifesto* (Harvard Business Press, 2009); Chris Laszlo, *Sustainable Value: How the World's Leading Companies Are Doing Well by Doing Good* (Stanford University Press, 2008).

23. Ben Webster, "IKEA's Claims on Wood Supply Do Not Stack Up," *Times* (London), March 12, 2011.

24. Many books review the reinforcing and escalating global environmental stresses from resource-intensive consumption. For a sampling of recent ones, see Gavin Bridge and Philippe Le Billon, *Oil* (Polity, 2012); Jennifer Clapp, *Food* (Polity, 2012); Michael Nest, *Coltan* (Polity, 2011); Elizabeth R. DeSombre and J. Samuel Barkin, *Fish* (Polity, 2011); Hellmuth Lange and Lars Meier, *The New Middle Classes: Globalizing Lifestyles, Consumerism, and Environmental Concern* (Springer, 2009).

25. Stacy Mitchell, *Walmart's Greenwash*, Institute for Local Self-Reliance, March 2012, as cited in Jennifer Ko, "Will Walmart Meet Its Sustainability Goals?" GreenBiz.com, March 8, 2012.

26. Beth Keck, comment at a Roundtable at Johns Hopkins School of Advanced International Studies, quoted in Sheldon Yoder, "Walmart's Sustainable Agriculture Strategy: A Model for the Private Sector and Sustainable Agriculture?" (Worldwatch.org, under "Nourishing the Planet").

27. Quoted in Simon Houpt, "And Now a Word (and Heck, Maybe the Plot) from Our Sponsor," *Globe and Mail*, May 7, 2011.

28. Peter Dauvergne, *The Shadows of Consumption: Consequences for the Global Environment* (MIT Press, 2008).

29. Quoted in Stephanie Rosenbloom and Michael Barbaro, "Green-Light Specials, Now at Wal-Mart," *New York Times*, January 25, 2009.

30. World Economic Forum, *The Consumption Dilemma*, section 1, executive summary.

Chapter 2

1. See, for example, Paul Hawken, *Blessed Unrest: How the Largest Movement in the World Came into Being and Why No One Saw it Coming* (Viking Penguin, 2007); Guha Ramachandra, *Environmentalism: A Global History* (Longman, 2000); Paul Wapner, *Living Through the End of Nature: The Future of American Environmentalism* (MIT Press, 2010).

2. For a history of the rise of corporate environmentalism, see Andrew J. Hoffman, *From Heresy to Dogma: An Institutional History of Corporate Environmentalism* (Stanford University Press, 2001).

3. For critical evaluations of corporate environmentalism in the 1990s, see Jed Greer and Kenny Bruno, *Greenwash: The Reality Behind Corporate Environmentalism* (Rowman and Littlefield, 1997); Sharon Beder, *Global Spin: The Corporate Assault on Environmentalism* (Scribe, 1997); Richard Welford, *Hijacking Environmentalism: Corporate Responses to Sustainable Development* (Earthscan, 1997); Andrew Rowell, *Green Backlash: Global Subversion of the Environmental Movement* (Routledge, 1996).

4. For a sampling of the literature on the firm-level politics of voluntary environmental compliance by corporations, see Aseem Prakash and Matthew Potoski, *The Voluntary Environmentalists: Green Clubs, ISO 14001 and Voluntary Environmental Regulations* (Cambridge University Press, 2006); Thomas Lyon and John Maxwell, *Corporate Environmentalism and Public Policy* (Cambridge University Press, 2004); Aseem Prakash, *Greening the Firm: The Politics of Corporate Environmentalism* (Cambridge University Press, 2000); Ronie Garcia-Johnson, *Exporting Environmentalism: US Multinational Chemical Corporations in Brazil and Mexico* (MIT Press, 2000).

5. For a recent critical analysis of the coopting and marketization of environmentalism, see Adrian Parr, *Hijacking Sustainability* (MIT Press, 2009). For a more optimistic account, see Michael Shellenberger and Ted Nordhaus, *Break Through: From the Death of Environmentalism to the Politics of Possibility* (Houghton Mifflin, 2007).

6. See, for example, Ellen Ruppel Shell, *Cheap: The High Cost of Discount Culture* (Penguin, 2009); Gordon Laird, *The Price of a Bargain* (McClelland & Stewart, 2009); Michael Andersen and Flemming Poulfelt, *Discount Business Strategy: How the New Market Leaders Are Redefining Business Strategy* (Wiley, 2006); Stanley D. Brunn, ed., *Wal-Mart World: The World's Biggest Corporation in the Global Economy* (Routledge, 2006); Charles Fishman, *The Wal-Mart Effect: How the World's Most Powerful Company Really Works—and How It's Transforming the American Economy* (Penguin, 2006).

7. Deloitte Touche Tohmatsu and STORES Media, *The Global Powers of Retailing* 2007 (Deloitte Touche Tohmatsu, 2007).

8. FundingUniverse, "The Gap, Inc." (available at http://www.fundinguniverse.com).

9. Deloitte Touche Tohmatsu and STORES Media, *Global Powers of Retailing 2012* (Deloitte Touche Tohmatsu, 2012), p. 10.

10. *Walmart Nation* is the title of a documentary film released in 2007 by Ultramagnetic Productions of Toronto.

11. Stacey Haas, Monica McGurk, and Liz Mhas, "A New World for Brand Managers," *McKinsey Quarterly*, April 2010, pp. 1–7.

12. Criteria for evaluating "the best" global brand include brand commitment, protection, clarity, responsiveness, authenticity, relevance, understanding, consistency, presence, and differentiation. See *Best Global Brands 2010* (Interbrand, 2010), pp. 6–9. See page 11 for an explanation of the brand value calculation (financial performance × role of brand × brand strength = brand value).

13. The estimate of the amount of traded timber now flowing through China is from William F. Laurance et al., "The Need to Cut China's Illegal Timber Imports," *Science Magazine* 29 (February) (2008), pp. 1184–1185. For reports and statistics on the illegal timber trade, see www.illegal-logging.info. For an analysis of the consequences of big-box retail and the globalization of supply chains on the world's forests, see Peter Dauvergne and Jane Lister, *Timber* (Polity, 2011).

14. There is a vast business literature on supply-chain logistics and risk management. On the nature and the complexities of fragment-

ing global production, see Jennifer Bair, ed., *Frontiers of Commodity Chain Research* (Stanford University Press, 2009); S. Tamer Cavusgil and Gary Knight, *Born Global Firms: A New International Enterprise* (Business Expert Press, 2009); Gary Gereffi and Miguel Korzeniewicz, *Commodity Chains and Global Capitalism* (Greenwood, 1994).

15. Frederick Mayer and Gary Gereffi, "Regulation and Economic Globalization: Prospects and Limits of Private Governance," *Business and Politics* 12, no. 3 (2010), p. 9.

16. Nelson Lichtenstein, *The Retail Revolution: How Wal-Mart Created a Brave New World of Business* (Metropolitan Books, 2009). One of Lichtenstein's current research projects is on "merchant capitalism."

17. World Economic Forum, "Global Risks" (available at http://www.weforum.org).

18. Roger Altman, "The Great Crash 2008: A Geopolitical Setback for the West," *Foreign Affairs*, January–February 2009, pp. 2–14.

19. For the idea of a "super cycle," see Roger Jones, "Commodity Super Cycle in Full Swing," *Financial Times*, February 1, 2011. On rising commodity prices, see *OECD-FAO Agricultural Outlook, 2010–2019* (OECD and FAO, 2010).

20. Quoted on the NRDC website (http://www.nrdc.org). Also see Frank Ackerman and Elizabeth A. Stanton, *The Cost of Climate Change* (NRDC, 2008), p. iv.

21. See, for example, Peter Utting, Darryl Reed and Ananya Mukherjee-Reed, eds., *Business Regulations and Non-State Actors: Whose Standards? Whose Development?* (Routledge, 2012); N. Craig Smith, C. B. Bhattacharya, David Vogel, and David Levine, eds., *Global Challenges and Responsible Business* (Cambridge University Press, 2010); Michael Hopkins, *Corporate Social Responsibility and International Development: Is Business the Solution?* (Earthscan, 2007).

22. See Homi Kharas and Geoffrey Gertz, *The New Global Middle Class: A Cross-Over from West to East* (Brookings Institution, 2010).

23. The Global Retail Development Index is based on mass merchant and food retailers and assesses the emerging market prospects in terms of 25 variables that include: economic and political risk, retail market attractiveness, retail saturation levels, modern retailing sales area, and sales growth. See A. T. Kearney, GRDI: A 10-Year Retrospective (available at http://www.atkearney.com).

24. Edelman Consulting, Purpose Bull Markets, Edelman goodpurpose® Study 2012 (available at http://www.purpose.edelman.com).

25. Source: "Unilever Unveils Plan to Decouple Business Growth from Environmental Impact," Unilever press release, November 15, 2010.

Chapter 3

1. World Business Council for Sustainable Development, *Vision 2050: The New Agenda for Business* (2010), p. 34.

2. Quoted in William McDonough and Michael Braungart, "The NEXT Industrial Revolution," *Atlantic Monthly* 282, no. 4 (October 1998).

3. See Stephan Schmidheiny with Business Council for Sustainable Development, *Changing Course: A Global Business Perspective on Development and the Environment* (MIT Press, 1992), p. 10. On eco-efficiency, see William McDonough and Michael Braungart, *Cradle to Cradle: Remaking the Way We Make Things* (North Point, 2002); World Business Council for Sustainable Development, *Eco-efficiency: Creating More Value with Less Impact* (2000); Livio DeSimone and Frank Popoff, *Eco-efficiency: The Business Link to Sustainability* (MIT Press, 2000). On eco-effectiveness, see McDonough and Braungart, "The Next Industrial Revolution," pp. 82–92. Alternatively, some companies also use the term "industrial ecology" to describe their closed-loop operational strategies to redefine waste by-products as useful inputs. See, for example, R. Socolow, C. Andrews, F. Berkhout, and V. Thomas, *Industrial Ecology and Global Change* (Cambridge University Press, 1994).

4. The FedEx eco-efficiency example is from Daniel C. Esty and Andrew S. Winston, *Green to Gold: How Smart Companies Use Environmental Strategy to Innovate, Create Value, and Build Competitive Advantage* (Yale University Press, 2006), p. 109. The Xerox eco-efficiency timeline is available at http://www.xerox.com. 3M's eco-efficiency estimates are available at http://solutions.3m.com.

5. The Walmart energy cost saving figure is from Michael Garry, "The Customer Drives IT Innovation at Wal-Mart," *Supermarket News*, January 25, 2010. The Yahoo estimate is from Andrew Winston, "A Portfolio of Green Strategies," at http://www.awarenessintoaction .com.

6. The Johnson & Johnson energy cost efficiency data are from Knut Haanaes et al., "Sustainability: The 'Embracers' Seize the Advantage," *MIT Sloan Management Review* 52 (3) (spring 2011), p. 8.

7. Ibid, p. 8.

8. US Environmental Protection Agency, *Report to Congress on Server and Data Center Energy Efficiency, Public Law 109–431*, ENERGY STAR Program, Washington, DC (August 2, 2007), p. 7.

9. Electric Power Research Institute, *Estimating the Costs and Benefits of the Smart Grid* (2011), p. 4-5.

10. The energy-consumption figure is from US Department of Energy, *Energy Efficiency Trends in Residential and Commercial Buildings*, October 2008, p. 9. The raw material usage figure is from David Malin Roodman and Nicholas Lenssen, *A Building Revolution: How Ecology and Health Concerns Are Transforming Construction*, Worldwatch Paper 124, Worldwatch Institute, 1995, p. 5.

11. Quoted in Janina Pfalzer, "IKEA to Build Wind Energy Park in Sweden to Power 17 Stores," Bloomberg.com, February 16, 2011.

12. Walmart, *2011 Global Responsibility Report*, p. 96.

13. Quoted in Chris Brown, "Key Takeaways from the Green Fleet Conference," *Business Fleet*, October 21, 2010.

14. Automotive Fleet, "Top 50 Green Commercial Fleets," *Automotive Fleet 500* 50, no. 5, 2011, pp. 28–29.

15. The Coca-Cola electric fleet estimates are from a Wharton interview with Coca-Cola Chairman and CEO John Brock (*Knowledge@Wharton*, http://knowledge.wharton.upenn.edu, December 23, 2008). The PepsiCo estimates are from Jim Motavalli, "Frito-Lay Adds Electric Trucks to Its Fleet," *New York Times*, September 8, 2010, and from the Frito-Lay press release "Frito-Lay Starts Charge on Largest Fleet of All-Electric Trucks in North America," September 8, 2010.

16. Ariela Abecassis, Jan Molina, and Aisha Tittle, *A Review of Water-Related Opportunities and Threats* (Marsh Canada, 2010), p. 2.

17. 2030 Water Resources Group, *Charting Our Water Future* (McKinsey & Company, 2009), p. 8.

18. The data on increasing water demand are from the Carbon Disclosure Project (CDP) Water Disclosure Project. For the statistics on water usage rates, see M. M. Mekonnen and A. Y. Hoekstra, *The Green, Blue and Grey Water Footprint of Crops and Derived Crop Products*, Value of Water Research Report Series No.47, UNESCO-

IHE, 2010. The comparative statistic on Coca-Cola's water usage is from Charles Fishman, *The Big Thirst: The Secret Life and Turbulent Future of Water* (Free Press, 2011), p. 120.

19. Fishman, *The Big Thirst*, p. 129.

20. Quoted in Andrew Shapiro, "Coca-Cola Goes Green," *Forbes*, January 29, 2010.

21. Summarized in John Elkington, "Unilever's Sustainability Living Plan Leads the Way: Is Unilever Too Ambitious?" *CSRwire*, November 18, 2010 (available at http://csrwiretalkback.tumblr.com).

22. Makower, *State of Green Business 2010*, p. 55.

23. See pp. 120–121 of "Save More. Live Better," a white paper by Walmart's senior vice-president of sustainability, Matt Kistler (available at http://www.awarenessintoaction.com).

24. Quoted in Shapiro, "Coca-Cola Goes Green."

25. Quoted in "Shareholder Resolutions Ask Major Packaged Goods Companies to Adopt Extended Producer Responsibility," As You Sow press release, April 28, 2011.

26. Quoted in Knut Haanaes et al., "Sustainability: The 'Embracers' Seize the Advantage," *MIT Sloan Management Review* 52 (3) (spring 2011), p. 25.

27. Heather M. Stapleton, Susan Klosterhau, Alex Keller, P. Lee Ferguson, Saskia van Bergen, Ellen Cooper, Thomas F. Webster, and Arlene Blum, "Identification of Flame Retardants in Polyurethane Foam Collected from Baby Products," *Environmental Science & Technology* 45 (12) (2011), pp. 5323–5331.

28. A. T. Kearney, "Green Winners: The Performance of Sustainability-focused Companies in the Financial Crisis," February 9, 2009. The study compares the market cap of 99 companies in the Dow Jones Sustainability Group Index with industry averages between May and November of 2008.

29. For an analysis of the growing preference of North American buyers for green purchasing, see TerraChoice Environmental Marketing Inc., *EcoMarkets Summary Report 2009*.

30. The eco-market and product statistics in this paragraph draw on the following: Jacquelyn Ottman, *The New Rules of Green Marketing: Strategies, Tools, and Inspiration for Sustainable Branding* (Berrett-Koehler, 2011); Kingfisher, *Strategic Update*, March 22, 2012;

McGraw-Hill Construction, *2011 Green Outlook: Green Trends Driving Growth* (2010); General Electric, *Ecomagination 2009 Annual Report 2009*, p. 9.

31. "All Eyes on Chinese Aisles," *The Economist*, May 21, 2011, p. 69; "Multinational Companies and China: What Future?" The Economist Intelligence Unit, December 07, 2011, pp.16-22. For more on Chinese consumerism, see Karl Gerth, *As China Goes, So Goes the World* (Hill and Wang, 2010); Tom Doctoroff, *Billions: Selling to the New Chinese Consumer* (Palgrave Macmillan, 2005).

32. Accenture, *Long-Term Growth, Short-Term Differentiation and Profits from Sustainable Products and Services* (2011), pp. 2, 9.

33. Quoted in Sindya N. Bhanoo, "Those Earth-friendly Products? Turns out They're Profit-friendly as Well," *New York Times*, June 12, 2010.

34. Ursula M. Burns and Anne M. Mulcahy, "Dear Stakeholders" letter, in Xerox's 2009 Report on Global Citizenship.

Chapter 4

1. Debra Hofman, Kevin O'Marah, and Carla Elvy, *The Gartner Supply Chain Top 25 for 2011* (Gartner, 2011), p. 3.

2. Michael Porter introduced the term "value chain" to refer to the economic gains as a product passes through each stage in the production chain, with the overall value greater than the sum of the parts. See Michael Porter, *Competitive Advantage: Creating and Sustaining Superior Performance* (Free Press, 1985). We use the overlapping terms "commodity chain" and "value chain" interchangeably with the term "supply chain." For an overview of the literature, see Jennifer Bair, ed., *Frontiers of Commodity Chain Research* (Stanford University Press, 2009); also see the Global Value Chain initiative at Duke University (available at http://www.globalvaluechains.org).

3. Emek Basker and Pham Hoang Van, "Imports 'Я' Us: Retail Chains as Platforms for Developing Country Imports," *American Economic Review* 100 (2), 2010, pp. 414–418.

4. On supply-chain "buyer power," see Gary Gereffi, "The Organization of Buyer-driven Global Commodity Chains: How US Retailers Shape Overseas Production Networks," in Gary Gereffi and Miguel Korzeniewicz, eds., *Commodity Chains and Global Capitalism* (Prae-

ger, 1994); Gary Gereffi, John Humphrey, and Timothy Sturgeon, "The Governance of Global Value Chains," *Review of International Political Economy* 12 (1) (2005), pp. 78–104; Nelson Lichtenstein, *The Retail Revolution: How Wal-Mart Created a Brave New World of Business* (Metropolitan Books, 2009).

5. Steve Lohr, "Stress Test for the Global Supply Chain," *New York Times*, March 20, 2011.

6. There is a large business literature on supply-chain risk management. See, for example, Teresa Wu and Jennifer Blackhurst, eds., *Managing Supply Chain Risk and Vulnerability: Tools and Methods for Supply Chain Decision-makers* (Springer, 2009); Gary S. Lynch, *Single Point of Failure: The Ten Essential Laws of Supply Chain Risk Management* (Wiley, 2009); George A. Zsidisin and Bob Ritchie, eds., *Supply Chain Risk: A Handbook of Assessment, Management, and Performance* (Springer, 2008); Donald Waters, *Supply Chain Risk Management* (Kogan Page, 2007).

7. For example, in 2006 Sony recalled 10 million computer battery packs that were at risk of catching fire, at a cost of as much as $250 million. In 2007, Mattel had to discard about $100 million worth of toys with lead paint.

8. US Immigration and Customs Enforcement, "Chinese Honey Importer Arrested for Allegedly Evading US Import Duties," press release, February 17, 2011; Jessica Leeder, "Honey Laundering: The Sour Side of Nature's Golden Sweetener," *Globe and Mail*, January 5, 2011. Also see Grace Pundyk, *The Honey Trail: In Pursuit of Liquid Gold and Vanishing Bees* (St. Martin's, 2010).

9. See, for example, Stephen Brammer, Stefan Hoejmose, and Andrew Millington, *Managing Sustainable Global Supply Chains: Framework and Best Practices* (Network for Business Sustainability, 2011); United Nations Global Compact and Business for Social Responsibility, *Supply Chain Sustainability: A Practical Guide for Continuous Improvement* (UN Global Compact Office, June 2010). For further readings, see Balkan Cetinkaya et al., *Sustainable Supply Chain Management: Practical Ideas for Moving Towards Best Practice* (Springer, 2011); Stuart Emmett and Vivek Sood, *Green Supply Chains: An Action Manifesto* (Wiley, 2010); Joseph Sarkis, ed., *Greening the Supply Chain* (Springer, 2006).

10. Quoted in Amy Cortese, "Friend of Nature? Let's See Those Shoes," *New York Times*, March 6, 2007.

11. See Christina Binkley, "How Green Are Your Jeans?" *Washington Post*, Classroom Edition, October 10, 2010.

12. Claudia Deutsch, "Greening the Supply Chains of Corporate America," *New York Times*, November 6, 2007.

13. Quoted in Binkley, "How Green Are Your Jeans?"

14. Arguably, eco-audits are limited because the primary goal is to improve the environmental performance of the corporate system, not the long-term integrity of a particular ecological system (e.g., protecting the biodiversity of a rainforest). In addition, the scale of supply chains and the scope of auditing itself further limit the capacity of auditing as a tool for managing ecological integrity, especially at a global scale.

15. For IKEA audit statistics, see *IKEA Sustainability Report 2010*, p. 60; *IKEA Sustainability Report 2011*, p. 28.

16. On the politics of transnational private governance authority, see Jane Lister, *Corporate Social Responsibility and the State: International Approaches to Forest Co-Regulation* (Vancouver, BC: UBC Press, 2011); Lars H. Gulbrandsen, *Transnational Environmental Governance: The Emergence and Effects of the Certification of Forests and Fisheries* (Elgar, 2010); Benjamin Cashore, Graeme Auld, and Deanna Newsom, *Governing through Markets: Forest Certification and the Emergence of Non-state Authority* (Yale University Press, 2004).

17. Gregory Unruh and Richard Ettenson, "Winning in the Green Frenzy," *Harvard Business Review*, November 2010, p. 113.

18. For more on eco-labeling, see Magnus Boström and Mikael Klintman, *Eco-standards, Product Labeling and Green Consumerism* (Palgrave Macmillan, 2008); Michael Conroy, *Branded! How the Certification Revolution Is Transforming Global Corporations* (New Society, 2007).

19. Quoted in "The Quest for Clean Supply Chains," GreenBiz.com, May 12, 2011.

20. As reported in Karen Weise, "The Race to Decide Who's Greenest," *Bloomberg*, November 29, 2011.

21. Craib Design & Communications and PricewaterhouseCoopers, *CSR Trends 2010* (2011), pp. 4, 42, 46.

22. A. T. Kearney, *Carbon Disclosure Project Supply Chain Report 2011* (Carbon Disclosure Project, 2011), p. 19.

Chapter 5

1. Quoted in Stephen Brammer, Stefan Hoejmose, and Andrew Millington, *Managing Sustainable Global Supply Chains: Framework and Best Practices* (Network for Business Sustainability, 2011), p.17.

2. Becky Quick, "Something's Gotta Give: As Commodity Costs Climb, Who Will Pay the Price?" *Fortune*, February 7, 2011, p. 56. For an assessment of the effects of resource scarcities on the fast-moving goods industry, see A. T. Kearney & World Resources Institute, *Rattling Supply Chains* (2008).

3. See "Coca-Cola's John Brock: Sustainability Is No Longer Niche," *Knowledge@Wharton*, December 23, 2008.

4. Gartner Inc., "Gartner Announces Rankings of Its 2011 Supply Chain Top 25," news release, June 2, 2011. For the detailed analysis, see Debra Hofman, Kevin O'Marah, and Carla Elvy, *The Gartner Supply Chain Top 25 for 2011* (Gartner, 2011).

5. "Rocks on the Menu," *The Economist Technology Quarterly*, March 12, 2011, p. 3.

6. Quoted in Alejandro Lazo, "Mars Sets Goal for Sustainable Cocoa Sources," *Washington Post*, April 10, 2009.

7. Ibid.

8. EIRIS, *A Drought in Your Portfolio: Are Global Companies Responding to Water Scarcity?* (2011).

9. By 2030, India's domestic water supply is likely to provide for only 50 percent of the country's total demand. See Hindustan Unilever, "Hindustan Unilever Launches 'India Water Body,'" press release, May 16, 2011.

10. See General Accounting Office, *Freshwater Supply: States' Views of How Federal Agencies Could Help Them Meet the Challenges of Expected Shortages*, Report to Congressional Requesters, July 2003.

11. Coca-Cola's water-stewardship programs are available at http://www.thecoca-colacompany.com.

12. See PepsiCo's inaugural water report, Water Stewardship: Good for Business. Good for Society, September 2010. See also Coca-Cola's first global water-stewardship report, Product Water Footprint Assessments: Practical Application in Corporate Water Stewardship, September 2010.

13. Todd Woody, "IBM Suppliers Must Track Environmental Data," *New York Times: Green* (a blog about energy and the environment), April 14, 2010, available at http://green.blogs.nytimes.com.

14. Beth Gardiner, "Beverage Industry Works to Cap Its Water Use," *New York Times*, March 22, 2011.

15. Quoted in A. T. Kearney, news release, "Greening the Supply Chain: Businesses Unlock Hidden Value," January 26, 2011.

16. Quoted in Ylan Q. Mui, "For Walmart, Fairtrade May Be More Than a Hill of Beans," *Washington Post*, June 12, 2006. For details of Nestlé's coffee plans, see Rainforest Alliance, "Rainforest Alliance Joins Nestlé in Plan to Transform Coffee Farming," press release, August 27, 2010.

17. IKEA, *IKEA Sustainability Report 2010*, p. 78.

18. Vikas Baja, "Cultivating a Market in India," *New York Times*, April 13, 2010.

19. Quoted in "Walmart Unveils Global Sustainable Agriculture Goals," Walmart news release, October 14, 2010. The impact of big brands on small farmers is an emerging, uncertain, and hotly debated topic. Interestingly, in a highly controversial late-2011 decision that was immediately revoked, the Indian government decided to open the country to large foreign retail companies, projecting overall benefits for Indian farmers. For the background analysis report that informed the government's decision, see Matthew Joseph, Niupama Soundararajan, Manisha Gupta, and Sanghamitra Sahu, *Impact of Organized Retailing on the Unorganized Sector* (Indian Council for Research on International Economic Relations, 2008).

20. Quoted in Suzanne Kapner, "Walmart Puts the Squeeze on Food Costs," *Fortune*, May 29, 2008.

21. Joseph Francis, *Supply Chain Management & Business Financial Performance*, presentation for the Supply Chain Council (http://supply-chain.org), July 25, 2010.

22. Quoted in Beth Kowitt, "Inside the Secret World of Trader Joe's," *Fortune*, August 23, 2010.

23. General Mills, 2010 GIS 10-K filing, p. 6.

24. Tadashi Yasui, *Custome Environmental Scan 2012* (World Customs Organization, 2012), p. 4; Leslie G. Brand, "EU Raids Shipping Companies in Anti-trust Probe," *Supply Chain Solutions*, May 17, 2011 (available at http://scs-logistics.net). For an overview of the po-

litical economy of shipping and international trade, see Peter Hall, Robert McCalla, Claude Comtois, and Brian Slack, eds., *Integrating Seaports and Trade Corridors* (Ashgate, 2011).

25. As cited in Larry Rohter, "Shipping Costs Start to Crimp Globalization," *New York Times*, August 3, 2008.

26. Summarized in David Street, "FMC Issues Notice of Inquiry on Slow Steaming" (available at http://shippersassociation.org).

27. Federal Maritime Commission, "FY 2012 Budget Estimates," submitted to Appropriations Committees of US Congress, February 14, 2011, p. 16.

28. See Clean Cargo Working Group, *Beyond the Factory Gates: How Brands Improve Supply Chain Sustainability through Shipping and Logistics* (Business for Social Responsibility, March 2011).

29. *Setting the Standard for Supply Chain Performance*, SAP White Paper, 2011, p. 1.

30. As quoted in Jo Bowman, "Topsy Turvy: Reorienting Supply and Demand," *Research World*, January–February 2011. Also see Rick Kash and David Calhoun, *How Companies Win: Profiting from Demand-Driven Business Models Regardless of What Business You're In* (HarperCollins, 2010).

31. There is a large and growing literature on consumers' demand for sustainable products and green marketing. See, for example, Al Iannuzzi, *Greener Products: The Making and Marketing of Sustainable Brands* (CRC Press, 2011); Jacquelyn Ottman, *The New Rules of Green Marketing: Strategies Tools and Inspiration for Sustainable Branding* (Greenleaf, 2011); Chris Arnold, *Ethical Marketing and the New Consumer* (Wiley, 2009); Neil Z. Stern and Willard N. Ander, *Greentailing and Other Revolutions in Retail: Hot Ideas That Are Grabbing Customer's Attention and Raising Profits* (Wiley, 2008); John Grant, *The Green Marketing Manifesto* (Wiley, 2007).

32. This estimate is based on a survey of more than 3,600 undergraduate and graduate students in more than 40 countries. See *Inheriting a Complex World: Future Leaders Envision Sharing the Planet* (IBM Institute for Business Value, 2010). See also Retail Customer Experience, *2011 Top 100: Retailers Issues and Trends That Are Making an Impact* (NetWorld Alliance, 2010).

33. Robert Monczka, John Blascovich, Leslie Parker, and Tom Slaight, "Value Focused Supply: Linking Supply to Business Strategies," *Supply Chain Management Review*, March–April 2011, pp. 46–54.

34. Bruce Temkin, *The Current State of Customer Experience* (Temkin Group, 2010), p. 14.

35. "SC Johnson Introduces Windex Mini, Hopes to Revolutionize Use of Cleaning Concentrates," news release, July 1, 2011.

36. Both quotes are from Paul Waldie and Carly Weeks, "Attention Shoppers: Walmart Plans to Offer Healthier Foods," *Globe and Mail*, January 21, 2011.

Chapter 6

1. Aron Cramer and Z. Karabell, *Sustainable Excellence: The Future of Business in a Fast-Changing World* (Rodale, 2010), pp. 103, 106.

2. Environmental Defense Fund, "Walmart: Our Seven Areas of Focus" (available at http://business.edf.org).

3. Al Gore, "Climate of Denial: Can Science and the Truth Withstand the Merchants of Poison?" *Rolling Stone*, June 22, 2011.

4. See, for example, "Measuring the Impact of Corporate Social Responsibility: Does CSR Matter?" (press release by the European Union's multi-partner IMPACT research project, July 23, 2010).

5. The literature on the relationship among power, legitimacy, and authority in global governance is vast. On power in this context, see James Scott, *Power* (Polity, 2001); Michael Barnett and Raymond Duvall, eds., *Power in Global Governance* (Cambridge University Press, 2005). On legitimacy (i.e., "the acceptance and justification of shared rule by a community" and "having the consent of the governed"), see Steven Bernstein and William Coleman, eds., *Unsettled Legitimacy: Power and Authority in a Global Era* (UBC, 2010); Steven Bernstein, "Legitimacy in Global Environmental Governance," *Journal of International Law and International Relations* 1 (1–2) (2005), pp. 139–166.

6. Joseph S. Nye Jr., *The Future of Power* (Public Affairs, 2011), p. xvii.

7. See Nike, "Letter from the CEO," *Corporate Responsibility Report 2007–09*, p. 5. On the growing importance of private authorities, complex public-private coalitions, and the participation of transnational actors in global governance more generally, see Shepard Forman and Derk Segaar, "New Coalitions for Global Governance: The Changing Dynamics of Multilateralism," *Global Governance* 12 (2)

(2006), pp. 205–225; Magdalena Bexell, Jonas Tallberg, and Anders Uhlin, "Democracy in Global Governance: The Promises and Pitfalls of Transnational Actors," *Global Governance* 16 (1) (2010), pp. 81–101.

8. Jason Clay, "Precompetitive Behaviour: Defining the Boundaries," *Guardian* Professional Network, June 2, 2011.

9. Quoted in Michael Burnham, "Another Utility Leaves U.S. Chamber Over Climate Policy," *New York Times*, September 25, 2009. A list of companies that oppose the US Chamber of Commerce's position on climate change is available at http://chamber.350.org.

10. For example, Greenpeace, Natural Resources Defense Council, the Sierra Club, and other environmental organizations have accused the American Forest & Paper Association of trying to lower the bar on the NGO-led Forest Stewardship Council's sustainable forest certification standard by developing and promoting a competing industry-initiated certification standard, the Sustainable Forest Initiative. In response, in March 2011 the AF&PA released *Better Practices, Better Planet 2020,* which they describe as "the most extensive and quantifiable set of sustainability goals for any major manufacturing industry in the U.S."

11. British Retail Consortium, *A Better Retailing Climate Progress Report 2010* (2010).

12. Grocery Manufacturers Association, *Reducing Our Footprint: The Food, Beverage and Consumer Packaging Industry's Progress in Sustainable Packaging* (2011); Consumer Electronics Association, *Inspiring Change: CEA 2010 Sustainability Report* (2010).

13. Quoted in "Consumer Goods Industry Announces Initiatives on Climate Protection," Consumer Goods Forum press release, November 29, 2010.

14. Nike Inc., *Corporate Responsibility Report 2007–09*, p. 23.

15. Neville Isdell, *Footprint. Handprint. Blueprint. How Business Can Tackle Climate Change*, June 12, 2009.

16. World Economic Forum, *Redesigning Business Value: A Roadmap for Sustainable Consumption* (2010), p. 15.

17. *Economist* Intelligence Unit, "Dangerous Liaisons: How Businesses Are Learning to Work with Their New Stakeholders" (2010), p. 8.

18. Quoted in Tobias Webb, "Does It Pay to Get in Bed with Business?" *Guardian*, February 25, 2005.

19. Environmental Leader, "Clorox Green Line Takes 42% of Natural Cleaners Market," January 13, 2009 (available at http://www.environmentalleader.com); Paul Rogers, "The Power of Green," *NYSEMagazine.com*, Q1 2010. Also see Christine MacDonald, *Green Inc.: An Environmental Insider Reveals How a Good Cause has Gone Bad* (Lyons, 2008).

20. Avrim Lazar, president and CEO of Forest Products Association of Canada, presentation to PricewaterhouseCoopers Global Forest and Paper Industry Conference, Vancouver, May 11, 2011.

21. Quoted in Oliver Balch, "Activist NGOs: Engage the Enemy More Closely?" *Ethical Corporation*, May 31, 2011.

22. Harris Gleckman, "Global Governance in a Globalized World: Global-Corporate-Alliances Have Eclipsed the Nation-State as the Key Institution of Global Governance," *Policy Innovations*, 2008, p. 14.

23. Quoted in Martin Wright, "Success Means Telling People to Buy Less," *Guardian Professional Network*, November 7, 2011.

24. See the 2011 Edelman Trust Barometer (available at http://www.edelman.com). One example of global corporate reputation tracking is the TNS Corporate Reputation Index.

25. Edward Humes, *Force of Nature: The Unlikely Story of Wal-Mart's Green Revolution* (HarperCollins, 2011).

26. For an analysis of consumer behavior toward sustainable products, see Tim Devinney, Pat Auger, and Giana Eckhardt, *The Myth of the Ethical Consumer* (Cambridge University Press, 2010).

27. Quoted in Lyndsey Layton, "Wal-Mart Turns to 'Retail Regulation,'" *Washington Post*, February 27, 2011, p. A04.

28. For example, China's Ministry of Science and Technology has a memorandum of understanding with Walmart for the company to roll out its environmental policies to its 20,000 suppliers across China to ensure legal compliance, greater transparency, higher product quality, and greater factory efficiency. China's Ministry of Environmental Protection has an agreement with Walmart to develop green supermarkets across the country. China's State Forest Administration has a memorandum of understanding with Walmart to promote forest certification in China.

29. Quoted in Peter Lacy, "Davos: Business Leaders Focus on 5 Sustainability Themes," *Bloomberg Business Week*, January 29, 2010.

30. Quoted in World Economic Forum, "Business Leaders Urged to Take Part in Greater Public-Private Cooperation to Strengthen Public Governance," press release, January 25, 2008.

31. World Business Council for Sustainable Development, *Vision 2050: The New Agenda for Business* (2010), pp. 1, 3.

32. Quoted in Catriona Davis, "Business 'Should Lead' on Global Warming, Says U.N. Climate Secretary," *CNN.com*, December 22, 2010.

33. Nestlé, *Nestlé Rural Development Report*, 2010, p. 61.

34. Greenpeace, "One Year After Nestlé Committed to Giving Rainforests a Break, What Has Been Achieved?" news release, May 23, 2011.

35. George Monbiot, "Ethical Shopping Is a Charade of the Rich," *Guardian Weekly*, 3 August 2007, p. 24.

36. See the Sierra Club Green Works webpage (available at http://www.sierraclub.org).

37. SERI research, as cited in World Economic Forum and Deloitte Touche Tohmatsu, *The Consumption Dilemma: Leverage Points for Accelerating Sustainable Growth*, 2011, p. 9.

38. World Economic Forum and Deloitte Touche Tohmatsu, *The Consumption Dilemma*, p. 9.

39. European Environment Agency, *Europe's Environment—The Fourth Assessment*, 2007, pp. 253, 322.

40. McKinsey, "Early Consumer Product Winners in the Developing World Could Score Lasting Gains," *McKinsey Quarterly*, September 2010; Business Monitor International, India Retail Report for second quarter of 2011 (available at http://www.ibef.org).

41. The concept of a rebound effect was introduced in 1865 by the economist Stanley Jevons. Referred to as the Jevons Paradox, it explains how improved resource efficiency (his example was coal) leads to increased consumption of the resource—canceling out the benefits of the efficiency gains. For readings, see John Polimeni, Kozo Mayumi, Mario Giampietro, and Blake Alcott, eds., *The Myth of Resource Efficiency: The Jevons Paradox* (UBC, 2009).

42. Sally Uren, Deputy Chief Executive, presentation at Forum for the Future Workshop, London, March 2010.

43. Peter Lacy, "Davos: Business Leaders Focus on 5 Sustainability Themes," *Business Week*, January 29, 2010.

Further Readings

Big Retail and the World Discount Economy

Peter Dauvergne and Jane Lister, *Timber* (Polity, 2011)

Lisa Ann Richey and Stefano Ponte, *Brand Aid: Shopping Well to Save the World* (University of Minnesota Press, 2011)

Nelson Lichtenstein, *The Retail Revolution: How Wal-Mart Created a Brave New World of Business* (Metropolitan Books, 2009)

Ellen Ruppel Shell, *Cheap: The High Cost of Discount Culture* (Penguin, 2009)

Gordon Laird, *The Price of a Bargain* (McClelland & Stewart, 2009)

Michael Andersen and Flemming Poulfelt, *Discount Business Strategy: How the New Market Leaders Are Redefining Business Strategy* (Wiley, 2006)

Stacy Mitchell, *Big-Box Swindle* (Beacon, 2006)

Stanley D. Brunn, ed., *Wal-Mart World: The World's Biggest Corporation in the Global Economy* (Routledge, 2006)

Charles Fishman, *The Wal-Mart Effect: How the World's Most Powerful Company Really Works—and How It's Transforming the American Economy* (Penguin, 2006).

Capitalism and Consumption

Peter Newell and Matthew Paterson, *Climate Capitalism: Global Warming and the Transformation of the Global Economy* (Cambridge University Press, 2010)

Richard H. Robbins, *Global Problems and the Culture of Capitalism*, fifth edition (Prentice-Hall, 2010)

David Harvey, *Enigma of Capital: and the Crisis of Capitalism* (Profile Books, 2010)

Peter Dauvergne, *The Shadows of Consumption: Consequences for the Global Environment* (MIT Press, 2008)

Matthew Paterson, *Automobile Politics: Ecology and Cultural Political Economy* (Cambridge University Press, 2007)

Thomas Princen, *The Logic of Sufficiency* (MIT Press, 2005)

Juliet B. Schor, *Born to Buy: The Commercialized Child and the New Consumer Culture* (Scribner, 2004)

Thomas Princen, Michael Maniates, and Ken Conca, eds., *Confronting Consumption* (MIT Press, 2002).

Competitive Advantages of Corporate Greening

C. B. Battacharyra, Sankar Sen, and Daniel Korschun, *Leveraging Corporate Responsibility: The Stakeholder Route to Maximizing Business and Social Value* (Cambridge University Press, 2011)

Edward Humes, *Force of Nature: The Unlikely Story of Wal-Mart's Green Revolution* (HarperCollins, 2011)

Chris Laszlo and Nadya Zhexembayeva, *Embedded Sustainability: The Next Big Competitive Advantage* (Greenleaf, 2011)

Aron Cramer and Z. Karabell, *Sustainable Excellence: The Future of Business in a Fast-Changing World* (Rodale, 2010)

Gil Friend, *The Truth About Green Business* (FT, 2009)

Adam Werbach, *Strategy for Sustainability: A Business Manifesto* (Harvard Business Press, 2009)

Joel Makower, *Strategies for the Green Economy: Opportunities and Challenges in the New World of Business* (McGraw-Hill, 2008)

Chris Laszlo, *Sustainable Value* (Stanford University Press, 2008)

Daniel Esty and Andrew Winston, *Green to Gold* (Yale University Press, 2006)

Bob Willard, *The Sustainability Advantage* (New Society, 2002).

Corporate Social Responsibility

Pratima Bansal and Andrew Hoffman, eds., *The Oxford Handbook of Business and the Natural Environment* (Oxford University Press, 2012)

Wayne Visser, *The Age of Responsibility: CSR 2.0 and the New DNA of Business* (Wiley, 2011)

Kurt Strasser, *Myths and Realities of Business Environmentalism: Good Works, Good Business, or Greenwash?* (Elgar, 2011)

Bryan Horrigan, *CSR in the 21st Century: Debates, Models and Practices across Government, Law and Business* (Elgar, 2010)

William Werther and David Chandler, *Strategic Corporate Social Responsibility: Stakeholders in a Global Environment* (Sage, 2010)

David Vogel, *The Market for Virtue: The Potential and Limits of Corporate Social Responsibility* (Brookings Institution, 2005).

Co-Regulation

Jane Lister, *Corporate Social Responsibility and the State: International Approaches to Forest Co-Regulation* (UBC, 2011)

Karin Bäckstrand, Jamil Khan, Annica Kronsell, and Eva Lövbrand, eds., *Environmental Politics and Deliberative Democracy: Examining the Promise of New Modes of Governance* (Elgar, 2010)

Josep M. Lozano, Laura Albareda, Tamyko Ysa, Heike Roscher, and Manila Marcuccio, *Governments and Corporate Social Responsibility: Public Policies Beyond Regulation and Voluntary Compliance* (Palgrave Macmillan, 2008)

Peter Glasbergen, Frank Biermann, and Arthur P. J. Mol, eds. *Partnerships, Governance and Sustainable Development* (Elgar, 2007)

Doreen McBarnet, Aurora Voiculescu, and Tom Campbell, eds., *The New Corporate Accountability: Corporate Social Responsibility and the Law* (Cambridge University Press, 2007)

Peter Utting and Jose Carlos Marques, eds., *Corporate Social Responsibility and Regulatory Governance: Towards Inclusive Development* (Palgrave Macmillan, 2010).

Eco-Certification

Lars H. Gulbrandsen, *Transnational Environmental Governance: The Emergence and Effects of the Certification of Forests and Fisheries* (Elgar, 2010)

Magnus Boström and Mikael Klintman, *Eco-Standards, Product Labelling and Green Consumerism* (Palgrave Macmillan, 2008)

Michael Conroy, *Branded! How the Certification Revolution Is Transforming Global Corporations* (New Society, 2007)

Aseem Prakash and Matthew Potoski, *The Voluntary Environmentalists: Green Clubs, ISO 14001 and Voluntary Environmental Regulations* (Cambridge University Press, 2006)

Benjamin Cashore, Graeme Auld, and Deanna Newsom, *Governing through Markets: Forest Certification and the Emergence of Non-State Authority* (Yale University Press, 2004).

Eco-Consumerism

Tim Divinney, Pat Auger, and Giana Eckhardt, *The Myth of the Ethical Consumer* (Cambridge University Press, 2010)

Hazel Henderson, *Ethical Markets: Growing the Green Economy* (Chelsea Green, 2006)

Rob Harrison, Terry Newholm, and Deirdre Shaw, *The Ethical Consumer* (Sage, 2005)

Michele Micheletti, *Political Virtue and Shopping: Individuals, Consumerism and Collective Action* (Palgrave Macmillan, 2003)

Michele Micheletti, *The Politics Behind Products: Using the Market as a Site for Ethics and Action* (Palgrave, 2003)

David Crocker and Toby Linden, *Ethics of Consumption: The Good Life, Justice, and Global Stewardship* (Rowman & Littlefield, 1998).

Eco-Efficiency

William McDonough and Michael Braungart, *Cradle to Cradle: Remaking the Way We Make Things* (North Point, 2002)

World Business Council for Sustainable Development, *Eco-Efficiency: Creating More Value with Less Impact*, 2000

Livio DeSimone and Frank Popoff with the World Business Council for Sustainable Development, *Eco-Efficiency: The Business Link to Sustainable Development* (MIT Press, 1997)

Stephan Schmidheiny with the Business Council for Sustainable Development, *Changing Course: A Global Business Perspective on Development and the Environment* (MIT Press, 1992).

Ethical Marketing

Al Iannuzzi, *Greener Products: The Making and Marketing of Sustainable Brands* (CRC Press, 2011)

Jacquelyn Ottman, *The New Rules of Green Marketing: Strategies Tools and Inspiration for Sustainable Branding* (Greenleaf, 2011)

Chris Arnold, *Ethical Marketing and the New Consumer: Marketing in the New Ethical Economy* (Wiley, 2008)

Neil Stern and Willard Ander, *Greentailing and Other Revolutions in Retail: Hot Ideas That Are Grabbing Customers' Attention and Raising Profits* (Wiley, 2008)

Kellie McElhaney, *Just Good Business: The Strategic Guide to Aligning Corporate Responsibility and Brand* (Berrett-Koehler, 2008)

John Grant, *The Green Marketing Manifesto* (Wiley, 2007).

Future of Environmentalism

Paul Wapner, *Living Through the End of Nature: The Future of American Environmentalism* (MIT Press, 2010)

Thomas Princen, *Treading Softly: Paths to Ecological Order* (MIT Press, 2010)

Christine MacDonald, *Green, Inc.: An Environmental Insider Reveals How a Good Cause Has Gone Bad* (Lyons, 2008)

Paul Hawken, *Blessed Unrest: How the Largest Movement in the World Came into Being and Why No One Saw It Coming* (Viking Penguin, 2007)

Michael Shellenberger and Ted Nordhaus, *Break Through: From the Death of Environmentalism to the Politics of Possibility* (Houghton Mifflin, 2007).

Global Supply-Chain Management

Balkan Cetinkaya et al., *Sustainable Supply Chain Management: Practical Ideas for Moving Towards Best Practice* (Springer, 2011)

Stuart Emmett and Vivek Sood, *Green Supply Chains: An Action Manifesto* (Wiley, 2010)

Jennifer Bair, ed., *Frontiers of Commodity Chain Research* (Stanford University Press, 2009)

S. Tamer Cavusgil and Gary Knight, *Born Global Firms: A New International Enterprise* (Business Expert Press, 2009)

Joseph Sarkis, ed., *Greening the Supply Chain* (Springer, 2006)

Gary Gereffi and Miguel Korzeniewicz, *Commodity Chains and Global Capitalism* (Greenwood, 1994).

Political Economy of Resource Consumption

Gavin Bridge and Philippe Le Billon, *Oil* (Polity, 2012)

Jennifer Clapp, *Food* (Polity, 2012)

Michael Nest, *Coltan* (Polity, 2011)

Elizabeth R. DeSombre and J. Samuel Barkin, *Fish* (Polity, 2011)

Charles Fishman, *The Big Thirst: The Secret Life and Turbulent Future of Water* (Free Press, 2011)

Jennifer Clapp and Peter Dauvergne, *Paths to a Green World: The Political Economy of the Global Environment*, second edition (MIT Press, 2011)

Karl Gerth, *As China Goes, So Goes the World: How Chinese Consumers Are Transforming Everything* (Hill and Wang/Farrar, Straus and Giroux, 2010)

Hellmuth Lange and Lars Meier, *The New Middle Classes: Globalizing Lifestyles, Consumerism, and Environmental Concern* (Springer, 2009).

Privatization of Global Environmental Governance

Jennifer Clapp and Doris Fuchs, eds., *Corporate Power in Global Agri-Food Governance* (MIT Press, 2009)

Peter Utting and Jennifer Clapp, eds., *Corporate Accountability and Sustainable Development* (Oxford University Press, 2008)

Robert Falkner, *Business Power and Conflict in International Environmental Politics* (Palgrave Macmillan, 2007)

Doris Fuchs, *Understanding Business Power in Global Governance* (Nomos, 2005)

David Levy and Peter Newell, eds., *The Business of Global Environmental Governance* (MIT Press, 2005).

Index

AIM-PROGRESS initiative, 157
Auditing, 102–105, 109, 155, 175

Better Cotton Initiative, 98, 102
Big boxes
  business model of, 14, 23, 36–41, 44, 131, 132
  formats of, 34, 35, 131, 132
Big brands
  legitimacy of, 137, 138, 179
  market concentration of, 34, 35, 38, 86
  power of, 86, 87, 111, 125–127, 155–157, 179
Branding, 24–27, 113, 114, 122–124
Brand value, 41, 168
Brazil, 18, 49, 50, 69, 70, 95, 118
British Retail Consortium, 142
Business for Social Responsibility, 139

Carbon accounting, 96, 97, 109, 141, 144, 153
Carbon Disclosure Project, 58, 59, 110, 123, 142, 151

Chemicals, toxic, 6, 45, 72, 73, 91, 102–104, 152
China, 9, 10, 14, 15, 18, 43, 47, 48, 51, 52, 79, 86, 89, 90, 104, 105, 116, 153, 181
Climate change, 46, 47, 58, 65, 123, 140, 147, 155, 156
Cloud computing, 60
Cocoa, 91, 92, 117, 118
Coffee, 123, 124, 133
Collusion, 22, 23, 128, 129
Commodity prices, 46, 47, 114–118
Conflict minerals, 92, 140, 141
Conservation International, 104, 147
Consumer approval, 129, 130, 149, 152, 157, 158
Consumer Goods Forum, 39, 100, 101, 143, 144
Container shipping, 127–129
Co-regulation, 152–154
Crowdsourcing, 130

Decoupling, 52, 159
Defective products, 87–93
Deforestation, 91, 101–105, 143, 156

Dodd-Frank Wall Street Reform and Consumer Protection Act, 92, 141

Earth Day, 30
Earth Summit, 6
Ecological protection, 30, 31, 66, 137, 158–160, 175
Ecological shadows, 25, 161
Ecological valuation, 115
Electric Power Research Institute, 61
Electric vehicles, 63, 64
Electronic Industry Citizenship Coalition, 92, 144
Emerging economies and markets, 9, 10, 49, 50, 78, 79
Energy conservation, 58–64
ENERGY STAR program, 60, 62, 107
Environmental Defense Fund, 20, 136, 149
Environmentalism, 32, 33, 52, 53
EPEAT, 60
European Environment Agency, 159
European Timber Retail Coalition, 102
European Union, 91, 92

Fair trade, 106, 123
Fleet management, 63, 64
Forest Footprint Disclosure Project, 100, 101, 142
Forest Stewardship Council, 106, 108
Forum for the Future, 149, 150, 160
Fossil fuels, 5, 58, 59, 83, 127, 128. *See also* Container shipping; Fleet management; Transport logistics
Friends of the Earth, 31

Global Ecolabelling Network, 106
Global economic challenges, 46, 154
Global Forest and Trade Network, 102
Global Reporting Initiative, 109, 142
Governance power, 16–21, 137, 138, 152–154
Green brands, 6, 75, 76, 150
Green chemistry, 74
Greenpeace, 20, 31, 73, 102–104, 147, 148, 149, 156, 180
Green procurement, 100–102, 153, 155
Green products, 56, 59, 75–78, 122, 123, 151, 158, 164
Greenwashing, 31, 109, 151

Higg Index, 99
Honey, 15, 89, 90, 116, 117

Incrementalism, 32, 53, 145, 146, 160
India, 17, 18, 49, 50, 119, 120, 125, 159, 176, 177
Ingredients, listing of, 74, 76, 122
International Business Leaders Forum, 139
International Corporate Achievement in Sustainable Development, 11
International Energy Agency, 48
International Green Award, 11

Labeling, 73–76, 89, 90, 99, 105–108, 129, 130, 150, 158
Lacey Act, 45, 91, 92
Leadership in Energy and Environmental Design, 61, 153
Lean manufacturing, 72
Life-cycle analysis, 96–99

Marine Stewardship Council, 101, 106, 118
Middle-class consumers, 48, 49, 78, 159

National Retail Federation, 141
Nature Conservancy, 104, 120, 121, 122
Non-governmental organizations, 19–22, 32, 33, 101–104, 146–149, 180

Offshore production, 88–90
Organic foods and other items, 32, 42, 75, 76, 77, 101, 106, 110, 123, 137
Outsourcing, 42

Packaging, 66–71
Partnerships, 19–22, 26, 27, 146–149
Price rollbacks, 3, 16, 125–127. *See also* Retail prices
Private labels, 14, 101, 122, 123, 129
Products
  certification of, 105–108
  downsizing of, 67–69
  lightweighting of, 67
  redesign of, 59, 77, 78, 156
Product Safety Law, 91
Purpose-driven strategies, 49–52

Rainforest Alliance, 105, 106, 117, 118, 123
Rare-earth metals, 10, 116
Rebound effect, 160, 182
Reputational legitimacy, 39, 102, 149–152, 181
Resource availability, 47, 48, 116, 118, 119
Responsible Sourcing Network, 109
Retail Industry Leaders Association, 141
Retail prices, reduction of, 125–127. *See also* Price rollbacks
Reverse logistics, 93

Shared value, 123
Sierra Club, 148, 158, 180
Slow steaming, 128, 129
Smaller-format retail locations, 132
Smart grids, 60, 61
Social media, 91, 109, 110, 131, 132
Social responsibility, corporate, 2–5
Solar energy, 59, 62, 78
Suppliers
  deceptive practices of, 16, 124
  scorecards for, 70, 71, 101, 102, 141, 155
Supply chain, 83, 84, 90–110, 113, 124, 125, 132–137, 156, 157
Sustainability Consortium, 96, 98, 144
Sustainability Index, 98, 99
Sustainability messaging, 51, 52, 122–125, 149–152
Sustainability reporting, 108–110

Sustainable Agriculture Initiative, 144, 145
Sustainable Apparel Coalition, 99, 144, 145
Sustainable development, 31, 32

Timber, illegal, 91, 91, 102, 105
Trade secrets, 14
Transformational change, 27, 32, 148
Transport logistics, 78, 127–129, 177, 178. *See also* Container shipping; Fleet management

UN Conference on Environment and Development, 31, 32
US Chamber of Commerce, 140, 141, 180
US Consumer Product Safety Commission, 91
US Environmental Protection Agency, 33, 61, 140, 149, 151, 152

Value chain, 11, 173. *See also* Supply chain

Water Disclosure Project, 64, 171
Water management, 64–66, 70, 71, 118–122
Wind energy, 62, 116
World Business Council for Sustainable Development, 55, 56, 139, 154
World Economic Forum, 26, 27, 46, 159
World Environment Center, 11, 124
World Resources Institute, 115
World Wildlife Fund, 19–21, 31, 105, 119, 120, 147, 149